Edited by Richard Atfield and Patsy Kemp

Enhancing the International Learning Experience in Business and Management Hospitality Leisure Sport Tourism

Threshold Press

First published 2008 by
Threshold Press Ltd
152 Craven Road
Newbury Berks RG14 5NR
Phone 01635-230272 and fax 01635-44804
email: publish@threshold-press.co.uk
www.threshold-press.co.uk

British Library Cataloguing in Publication Data
A catalogue record for this book is available from the British Library

ISBN 978–1–903152–23–2

Printed in England by Biddles Ltd, Kings Lynn

Every effort has been made to trace the copyright holders and we apologise in
advance for any unintentional omissions. The editors and the publisher would be
pleased to insert the appropriate acknowledgement in any subsequent edition.

The editors

Richard Atfield is Academic Developer for the Business Management Accountancy
and Finance Subject Centre. He has a strong interest in internationalisation and
has established a special interest group in the area for BMAF, as well as forming
links with universities overseas. His career spans management and workforce
development in the NHS and lecturing in the UK and Hong Kong for Oxford
Brookes University.

Patsy Kemp has experience of working in education and training across the globe. As
Academic Developer for the Higher Education Academy Network for Hospitality,
Leisure, Sport & Tourism, she works to support practitioners in their roles with
Higher Education.

Contents

Introduction

Enhancing the International Learning Experience is timely: preparing learners to work effectively across cultures in a context of global employability is something that cannot be ignored. If we aim to deliver an educational experience which is fit for purpose in the 21st century, then we have to develop our approaches to meet the challenges imposed by internationalisation, globalisation, and all that goes with the claim of being international or world-class – 'business as usual' is not an option. If we pay lip service, as De Vita and Case (2003) suggest many do, or assume that the mere presence of international students is what constitutes international and fail to adapt learning, teaching and assessment practices to reflect internationalisation and a more inclusive pedagogy, then we run the risk not only of being arrogant but of failing to recognise the fundamental nature of the challenge and thereby short-changing *all* our students.

The Higher Education Academy (the Academy) recognises the importance of internationalisation as a key part of its activity. The internationalisation section of the Academy website articulates a commitment to support initiatives that enhance the student experience identifying the breadth of the focus:

○ curriculum development to prepare all graduates, regardless of country of origin, to be informed, responsible citizens able to work effectively in a global, multicultural context

○ development of initiatives to enhance the learning experience of international students

○ supporting the sector in engaging with the Bologna process (http://www.heacademy.ac.uk/ourwork/learning/international)

These issues are particularly pertinent to the Business Management Accountancy and Finance (BMAF) and the Hospitality Leisure Sport and Tourism (HLST) subject centres' communities, whose provision attracts a high proportion of international students. They are engaged with a substantial number of international partners (through collaborative agreements and franchised programmes) and their graduates enter occupations that are inescapably global. What is more, baseline surveys of deans and key contacts reveal that internationalisation is highlighted as a top-five priority.

While some of the importance of internationalisation unavoidably has its roots in the financial imperative, substantial drivers have included the need to respond to the challenges posed by increased numbers of international students, the complexity of engaging with international partnerships and the fact that increased international competition, means that we have to up our game in terms of the student experience

(Fielden, 2006). Add to this the public profile that student satisfaction (or lack of it) attracts, coupled with the rising importance of the employability agenda, and employers' demands for graduates with a 'broader world view' who are 'cross-culturally competent' (Shiel et al, 2005; Gillingham, 2006), then internationalisation and all that goes with it becomes naturally a critical priority.

This is all very well, some might say, but what else are we expected to do? Surely we are already doing enough, to address these issues? Evidence suggests not (Gillingham, 2006). While most of our institutions will have strategies for internationalisation, few have fully got to grips with its implications in the broadest sense or appreciate that it is not a peripheral activity (Luker, 2006) but pervades all aspects of university life. 'Internationalising the curriculum' as 'a relatively new phenomenon' (Caruana and Hanstock, 2008) presents a much more challenging task (Ritchie, 2006) that is often deferred or poorly addressed. Some of us will undoubtedly be further along in the 'process' (de Wit and Knight, 1995) of internationalising but judging by the number of attendees at recent Subject Centre events and the concerns raised at internationalisation workshops, there is a real demand to learn more. This is where this publication makes an early and important contribution: it provides an outline for mapping the terrain, shares activity from across the subject provision and explores the issues from a variety of perspectives. Internationalisation might not bite in exactly the same way at the programme level across all BMAF and HLST provision (some programmes are by nature of their discipline inherently more international), but there are enough similarities to suggest that alignment of effort makes sense: the learning is transferable. The centres are to be applauded for their initiative: they are tackling internationalisation and, by sharing scarce resource, are addressing the need for sustainable development (another sector priority) from the ground up.

Initiatives targeted at international students are obviously an important consideration and have been the starting point from which many institutions have developed a research interest, shedding light on the international student experience. Such a starting point is hardly surprising: international students have made an important contribution to UK higher education (predicted to rise to £20 billion by 2020) and particularly to business and management provision. In a highly competitive market, if we do not address the concerns of international students and enhance their learning experience, the consequences impact upon recruitment and retention, not to mention damaged reputation.

But there is something that we have to consider – should this focus be any different to the quality assurance and enhancement process that is at the heart of educational practice? The argument that international students are paying fees so 'we should do more for them' was the rationale for placing a spotlight on their experience in the past, but does that logic still hold currency? Most students now pay fees so under the banner of equality and inclusivity too much of a focus on the international student population might distract (or even detract) from developing the wider internationalisation agenda. Luker suggests that 'true internationalisation requires looking at the student body as a whole, not as several distinct populations' (Luker, 2008: 13). He also reinforces the notion that internationalisation is pervasive and thus, 'cannot be a peripheral activity' (Luker, 2006: 3), so a more holistic approach merits consideration.

A number of universities (including my own) have sought to develop a broader approach, attempting to locate internationalisation under the strategic umbrella of developing global perspectives and global citizenship across the institution (Shiel & McKenzie, 2008; Jones & Brown, 2007; Lunn, 2006). Such approaches offer strategic benefits, in that they address the 'internationalisation at home' agenda while at the same time enhancing the experience of both UK and international students. They also provide an organising framework for integrating other strategic imperatives such as, for example: international partnerships; international research; community engagement and volunteering in both the local and global spheres; and even the institutional equality and diversity agendas. The first case study by Elspeth Jones provides a cogent summary of one such approach, illustrating the breadth of what might be involved. This case sets the goalposts high, describing a strategic institutional approach to internationalisation, which extends beyond the recruitment of international students to permeate all aspects of campus life at Leeds Met University – an institution a long way down the road of internationalisation. This commitment to developing global perspectives begins with setting a vision and values that embrace the curriculum, the student experience (home and overseas) and the extra-curricular. The approach is resulting in culture change and contributing to enhancing the learning and experience of all students and staff.

Jude Caroll's case study puts the focus firmly onto one of the core components of what we do: assessment. Mention 'assessment' in a conversation which includes 'international' and very soon someone will be talking about plagiarism. It would not be uncommon for the conversation then to veer to the problems international students have with assessment. Before long the discussion has lapsed into a 'deficit model' of international students and how they do not seem to understand how to cite academic work. Caroll's paper makes an important contribution in the sense that it reminds us that perceptions of assessment and plagiarism are culturally situated: both students and teachers need to adjust and adapt (the former to secure success and the latter to establish more inclusive assessment practices and to help students manage transitions). The case study serves as a useful reminder of what we should be doing, irrespective of the nationality of learners, as part of what constitutes good educational practice. An aide-memoire on setting assessments and plagiarism, or more correctly, how to set them to reduce plagiarism, is provided.

International partnerships offer one vehicle for developing the cross-cultural capability of staff. In the third case study, Sandie Randall shares learning from Queen Margaret University, providing an account of the institution's approach to international collaborative partnerships and in particular, the School of Business Enterprise and Management's experience (gained over a 10-year period) with partners in India. The case study sets out the challenges, describes important learning points from their experience and usefully reminds us that shared commitment and mutual respect are essential (but too often forgotten) elements in the development of international partnership. I found this reminder refreshing: in the early days of internationalisation and forays abroad reciprocity in learning was often not high on the agenda – if it was considered at all.

Elspeth Jones, towards the end of her case, highlights the importance of 'firing imaginations and offering life changing experiences'. If such heady stuff leaves the reader inspired but wondering how to take this forward, then the contribution from Nina Becket and Maureen Brookes offers a step back to firmer ground and practical suggestion. The authors, like Jones, outline various dimensions of internationalisation (curriculum, student experience, recruitment, partnerships, exchanges, research and alumni relations) then go on to demonstrate how these can function as a practical tool to evaluate the extent of internationalisation. They deploy their framework across a sample of UK hospitality management programmes. One suggestion they make is that more opportunities to extend the international experience of UK students (and staff) would contribute to enhance the internationalisation of hospitality undergraduate degrees. While visiting other countries is of value, given that resources (financial and time) often militate against study abroad, what seems important is that we explore other ways to develop cross-cultural understanding and capability.

An important aspect of developing a global perspective is the ability to challenge our own assumptions and a preparedness to engage with opportunities that enable us to look through an alternative cultural lens. The next case study from a French business school (but perhaps not a typical *grande école*) offers just that, providing insight into teaching and learning issues in a context where cultural diversity (of students and staff) is more extreme than many of us will experience and where the administrative system serves as a brake on innovation and change. What's more Alan Darricote and Rod McColl, in a very honest and critical account, provide an illustration of a strategic approach to internationalisation. They highlight change-management issues in the development process of the school and the challenges encountered. Their paper is proffered as a basis to engage others in discussion and debate. The multi-cultural context they describe offers an exciting milieu for research from a dual perspective: enhancing international education and also international education management and administration.

In contrast to the strategic consideration in the previous case, Jan Bamford shifts the focus reminding us of the centrality of the student. The case study shares empirical data, in the form of focus groups and interviews, to draw attention to how international students perceive their experience. The experience for some students, particularly those at the baseline of language ability, is stressful. This is matched by frustration on the part of those students who are more linguistically advanced – and yet language and study support provided is often generic in nature. The case outlines the range of support required to help students adjust to a different academic regime and new social/cultural setting. Building support for all students is a critical process. However, a recurrent theme for international students is their sense of isolation: socialisation does not happen by chance. This reinforces what ISB (International Student Barometer)[1] data frequently reveals across many institutions: international students cite a lack of mixing with UK students. Practical solutions include the provision of a mentor, study-skills groups and conversation groups. The case makes the important reminder of the potential of cultural diversity to enrich learning – we need to develop staff and approaches to tap into this.

Mari Jo Pesch offers an American perspective on cultural diversity, describing how Marian College Wisconsin has adopted a global perspective as a framework for managing diversity, developing cultural sensitivity and enhancing the student learning experience. Although the faculty are in the early stages of this development, attention is drawn again to something that we all need to consider in taking this agenda forward – challenging our own assumptions is a first and essential step in developing an inclusive pedagogy. This is critically important to internationalisation: an Anglo-Saxon, or even a Eurocentric, perspective may not always lead to the best solution.

An industry where a multi–cultural perspective would seem to be pre-requisite is hospitality leisure and tourism. The case study by Judie Gannon addresses the international nature of the industry and the extent to which the international skills that the industry espouses as necessary for recruitment are developed within educational programmes. This is an interesting study which highlights that, despite what we may intuitively feel should be the situation (inter-cultural competence is necessary for managers in this industry), evidence gathered relating to recruitment processes reveals that recruiters demonstrate a limited understanding of concepts such as cultural sensitivity and inter-cultural skills. On the other side of the coin, research into how these issues are covered in the curriculum reveals a patchy picture in terms of the attention paid to offering learners an international experience and developing intercultural competence within programmes.

A perspective into how a truly international programme might be developed is offered by Melanie Weaver, Angela Vickerstaff and Malcolm Sullivan in the next case. They describe the course-development process for a masters in marketing targeted specifically at an international audience. They outline the research that informed the development and validation of a programme that might more effectively meet the needs of a culturally diverse group. They describe the principles, highlight the needs of international students and offer insight into course development and evaluation. Important reminders include that it is too easy to see 'overseas' as a homogenous

1 http://www.i-graduate.org/services/student_barometer.html

group and that an enhanced learning experience is more likely with a non-traditional form of delivery and higher student/staff ratios. Many of us would support the latter (we could all do more within a bigger resource envelope): the challenge is to explore non-traditional approaches within resource constraints.

Resource constraints have in part contributed to a rise in the use of group work as a form of assessment, giving rise to concerns (and complaints from students) about how to ensure that all members contribute (and if they don't does it matter?) but more importantly, how to ensure fair assessment. The academic rationale for collaborative learning through group work is undoubted but how do we address students' concerns, particularly where there are strong perceptions that marks will be 'pulled down' by weaker students. Rachel Wicaksono sheds light on these issues providing a summary of very detailed research focused specifically on group assessment at the undergraduate level. She explores the issues thoroughly, developing a conceptual framework from the literature and incorporating concepts of self-identity and self-categorisation theory. Her study is not conclusive in terms of the negative impact of group work on marks but does confirm the benefits of group work. The author provides a useful outline of considerations.

The case study from Philip Warwick confirms the importance of listening to international students and ensuring that they are given a voice. Warwick describes the 'annual listening survey' and an action-research approach that involves seeking feedback from masters level students to inform change in a context of rapid growth of international student numbers and in particular, Chinese students. The case highlights the issues that many readers will be familiar with and usefully reminds us that a process of continual enhancement is important if we expect learners to recommend their experience to others.

Jacqueline Lynch's case study outlines a post-graduate module undertaken by an internationally diverse student cohort, where learners are required to engage with reflective practice and consider learning styles. This paper seems to highlight what Dewey (1933) suggested – reflection by its very nature involves a painful process which includes puzzlement and doubt. It is thus hardly surprising that reflective practice presents a challenge to most students although some (depending on where they undertook their first degree) will be influenced by prior expectations and thus, more likely to adopt a mechanistic approach. While the case does not provide conclusions on cross-cultural differences, it does highlight the benefits gained by participants of multi-cultural working and the insight gained from understanding learning styles.

The case study by Rong Huang offers an interesting slant on what I have already referred to as the rhetoric of the 'deficit model' where international students are berated for not matching our cultural expectations: 'lack of critical thinking ability' is part of the language of this negative view. Huang provides food for thought through an exploration of what lies behind this accusation. In a limited study of postgraduates she delves into Chinese students' perceptions of critical thinking. This is nicely offset by an exploration of how UK academics define critical thinking – not surprisingly academics do not speak with one voice in defining what is meant by the term. If we do not share an understanding of what is a common term, is it any surprise that students are confused? Although Huang cautions that the sample is too limited to extrapolate (a small sample of Chinese students on a postgraduate hospitality management course), the reader is left thinking that these issues will be the same across the sector. The case study is an important reminder that we need to deconstruct our own practice. It reinforces for me personally what was suggested by De Vita and Case (2003) that internationalisation should be seen as the chance 'to reflect on, and rethink, not only what we teach but also how we teach.'

The case study from Mike Lowe highlights something that needs further rein-forcement: international students are a valuable resource in terms of the knowledge, cultural richness and diversity of experience that they bring to the learning environ-ment. The potential to exploit this is largely untapped. The case provides an honest account of the early experiences with Hong Kong students and the 'critical incidents' on the BA (Hons) Leisure Management extension degree with the steps that were taken to address the problems encountered. The experience of evaluators over a timeline is presented and a conceptual link is made with relationship marketing: we are reminded how relationships are nurtured over time.

The final case study reminds us that an important aspect of the 'internationalisa-tion at home' agenda is to find ways to broaden the horizons of UK students through international exchange and experiencing diversity 'outside the nation state' (Stier, 2002; Caruana and Hanstock, 2005). However, getting UK students to leave their comfort zones is something that presents a very real challenge, as any ERASMUS coordinator will confirm – perhaps a partial explanation to why there is a paucity of literature on UK students abroad (Caruana and Hanstock, 2008). Sandra King's study therefore is most welcome, describing something that is both unusual and innovative – an evaluation of a study visit to China, setting out the problems experi-enced and the benefits gained. This case will hopefully serve to inspire others to con-sider what might be possible: how do we build in opportunities to increase exposure to a very different culture with the potential to enhance learning from (and indeed empathy with) a radically different perspective. At a time when fewer UK students study languages, and unfortunately fewer programmes support language learning, building study visits into course development becomes a greater challenge.

I would like to thank all of the contributors for sharing their insight and expe-rience. Collectively these very different contributions reinforce the importance of developing this agenda. The publication provides substantial evidence of the genuine efforts of educators across the sectors in getting to grips with internationalisation in all its various guises. Through highlighting the variety of avenues to be followed (from the top-level strategic approach down to issues at the coal face and particular learning and teaching practices), the outcome is a useful resource, which lends itself to suggestions for future developments and research.

Clarke (2008) at the Academy conference reminded participants that there is often an imbalance (evident at the conference) manifesting itself by too much of a tendency to focus on international students, with insufficient attention given to UK students and internationalising for 'non-mobility'. He also stressed the importance of the extra-curricular sphere as a site of learning, outlining the role of the Student's Union and bodies such as U8[2]. This publication attempts to redress that imbalance in terms of perspectives: a few cases have indeed focused solely on international students but in most cases learning has been extended to consider broader issues. In moving forward and in developing the research agenda, we need to be cautious: the issues of international students should not be seen as too distinctively different to the issues of all students. Rather their concerns should act as a trigger to inform the enhancement of practice across the board. That is not to deny the importance of giving international students a voice but perhaps we should also seek the voice of UK students – why are they reluctant to undertake overseas study and do they fully appreciate, for example, that ability to communicate across cultures and exhibit a 'worldview' is valued by employers?

Killick (2006) stresses the importance of UK students developing cross-cultural capability suggesting that 'whether good citizens or bad, they cannot continue to live as little islanders' – but do they realise the extent to which the presence of international students offers a valuable learning opportunity – and as academics, can we honestly say that our learning, teaching and assessment practices fully encourage students to learn from multiple cultural perspectives? Do they develop more global perspectives as a consequence of the experience we provide? These are important questions to consider.

In a crowded curriculum, working in the extra-curricular sphere (as Clarke suggests) may well be one vehicle to address 'citizenship' and a way to hone the skills 'to work effectively in a global, multi-cultural context' but this gives rise to further questions, which merit a detailed exploration. For example, how does the extra-curricular contribute to the student learning experience and internationalisation? What evidence is there of practice which successfully aligns the extra-curricular with the taught curriculum? More importantly, how do we encourage students to see the value of extra-curricular learning for their development and preparation for global employability?

Such questions highlight only a few of the issues that need to be considered[3] – unfortunately, there are no simple solutions, but it is heartening that the Subject Centres are working together to provide a forum for sharing approaches. As others have suggested, internationalisation is complex and involves a long journey; at its

2   http://www.u8development.com/

3   The Literature Review on Internationalisation by Caruana and Spurling (2007), pp78-80 identifies 'substantial gaps' in the literature which offer ideas for developing the research agenda

heart is the process of learning and enhancement. This publication provides a basis for both. What seems critically important is that we strive to ensure that when we say our programmes, our faculties and our business schools are international, they are truly international. Only when an international outlook pervades everything that we do, can we say that we make an effective contribution to global education. Let's prepare our students to work in a world that we want to inhabit – we may need to deconstruct our own practice first but we stand to gain in the process.

References

Clarke, J. (2008) Internationalisation at home: students as global citizens. Paper presented at HE Academy Conference: Transforming the student experience

Caruana, V. and Hanstock, J. (2005) Internationalising the Curriculum – Initial Forays. Graduates as Global Citizens: Education for Sustainable Development, 1st International Conference, Bournemouth University, September

Caruana, V. and Hanstock, J. (2008) Internationalising the curriculum at the University of Salford: from rhetoric to reality. In *The Global University the role of senior managers*. BU/DEA: www.dea.org.uk/publications pp 31–5

Caruana, V. and Spurling, N. (2007) *The Internationalisation of UK Higher Education: A review of selected material*. Available at http://www.heacademy.ac.uk/ourwork/learning/international

Clarke, J. (2008) Internationalisation at home: students as global citizens. HE Academy Annual Conference, July. Available at http://www.heacademy.ac.uk/resources/

De Vita, G. and Case, P. (2003) Rethinking the internationalisation agenda in UK higher education. *Journal of Further and Higher Education* 27 (4) pp 383–98

Dewey, J. (1933) *How We Think: A restatement of the relation of reflective thinking to the educative process*

Fielden, J. (2006) *Internationalisation and Leadership: What are the issues? Leadership Summit 2006: The Leadership Challenges of Globalisation and Internationalisation*. Available at www.lfhe.ac.uk/international/summit2006/

Gillingham, D. (2006) Business schools in the global marketplace. *academy exchange* 5 Winter pp 26–7. Available at http://www.heacademy.ac.uk/resources/

Jones, E. and Brown, S. (eds) (2007) *Internationalising Higher Education*. London: Routledge

Killick, D. (2006) The internationalised curriculum. *academy exchange* 5 Winter pp 13–15

Knight, J. & De Wit, H. (1995) Strategies for internationalisation of higher education: historical and conceptual perspectives. In H. De Wit (ed) *Strategies for Internationalisation of Higher Education: A Comparative study of Australia, Canada and the United States of America*. Amsterdam: EAIE

Luker, P. (2006) Not yet Prime Minister. *academy exchange* 5 Winter pp 13–15

Luker, P (2008) The internationalising of Higher Education: shifting the paradigm. In *The Global University the role of senior managers*. BU/DEA: www.dea.org.uk/publications pp 11–14

Ritchie, E. (2006) Internationalisation: where are we going and how do we know when we have got there? *academy exchange* 5 Winter pp 13–15

Lunn, J. (2006) *Global Perspectives in higher education*. The Royal Geographical Society with IBG

Shiel, C. (2006) Developing the Global Citizen. *academy exchange* 5 Winter pp 18–20

Shiel, C. and McKenzie, A. (eds) (2008) *The Global University: the role of Senior Managers*. BU/DEA: www.dea.org.uk/publications

Shiel, C., Williams, A. and Mann, S. (2005) Global Perspectives and Sustainable Development in the Curriculum: Enhanced Employability, More Thoughtful Society? in *Enhancing Graduate Employability: The roles of learning, teaching, research and knowledge transfer, Proceedings of the Bournemouth University Learning and Teaching Conference*, Bournemouth University

Stier, J. (2002) Internationalisation in higher education: unexplored possibilities and unavoidable challenges. European Conference on Educational Research, 11–14 September, Lisbon, available at http:// www.leeds.ac.uk/educol/documents/00002342.htm

CHRIS SHIEL has almost 20 years experience in business and management education having started her career as the course leader for the BABS degree at Bournemouth University. In that time she has undertaken a number of business school roles including Head of Programmes, Head of HRM and Head of Learning and Teaching. She has also contributed to the development of international recruitment and partnerships, with extensive experience in the Far and Middle East. Since 1999 she has led the development of Global Perspectives at Bournemouth University and a number of e-learning initiatives including developing the first e-learning Foundation Degree for the Armed Forces. In 2005, she was awarded a Leadership Foundation Fellowship for her work; this enabled her to develop a strategic approach for developing the 'education for sustainable development: graduates as global citizens' agenda. She has contributed to of a number of publications including, in 2008, *The Global University: the role of senior managers* (funded by HEFCE). She has recently moved from the business school to become Director of the Centre for Global Perspectives, with an institution-wide remit to contribute to internationalisation and the development of graduates who are better prepared for global employability.

World-wide horizons at Leeds Metropolitan University

Elspeth Jones
Leeds Metropolitan University

Changing the culture of an organisation as large as a
university is not easy, but this is exactly what Leeds Metropolitan
has been doing to support internationalisation.

Introduction

Since 2003 we have engaged the staff and student community in enriching the learning experience for both home and international students and to expand staff horizons. Our strategic approach reflected the institution's values and re-framed our recruitment of international students within a broader ethical context. While universities vary in the degree to which they view internationalisation as a 'whole of institution' initiative (Knight, 2007), Fielden claims that the trend is for internationalisation strategies in UK universities to become 'more all-embracing and to require the involvement of all the community' (Fielden, 2008: 1). It may be timely therefore to offer Leeds Metropolitan's experience as an illustration for those universities adopting a similar strategy or considering an institutional commitment to global perspectives across the curriculum.

Developing world-wide horizons

In a recent publication on the role of senior managers in internationalising higher education, Shiel suggests that universities are uniquely placed to contribute to internationalisation and sustainable development and argues that both concepts combine in the term 'global perspectives' (Shiel, 2008: 7). In 2003, Leeds Metropolitan began to broaden its approach to internationalisation, moving away from profit-oriented international student recruitment and towards one which better reflected institutional values. It sought to develop global perspectives, or 'world-wide horizons' across the staff and student body. Our Vision and Character Statement (Leeds Metropolitan, 2006) characterises Leeds Metropolitan as striving to be 'a world-class regional university with world-wide horizons, using all our talents to the full'. One of the ten statements of vision and character shows that we intend to be:

> a university with world-wide horizons where an international, multicultural ethos is pervasive throughout our scholarship, curriculum, volunteering and community engagement at home and overseas.   (Leeds Metropolitan, 2006: Aim 9)

This required radical reconsideration of all aspects of the university's life and work if we were to achieve the

> ongoing, future oriented, multi-dimensional, interdisciplinary, leadership-driven vision that involves many stakeholders working to change the internal dynamics of an institution to respond and adapt appropriately to an increasingly diverse, globally-focused, ever-changing external environment.   (Ellingboe, 1998: 199)

An international faculty and international dean were created, with the faculty responsible for fostering and leading internationalisation across the university. A group of cognate subjects with broadly international themes, such as tourism, languages, hospitality and events, were brought together in the faculty. In addition, new subject areas were developed, and a School of Applied Global Ethics was created to offer courses such as Development studies and Peace and conflict resolution. A further focus of the faculty's work was to promote international understanding and develop global perspectives across the curriculum for all students across the university, both home and international. Alongside this, the faculty would also lead on developing the world-wide horizons of staff.

Internationalisation 2003–08

Our holistic view for the 2003 internationalisation strategy was based on the widely-used definition of internationalisation, 'the process of integrating an international/intercultural dimension into the teaching, research and service of an institution' (Knight and de Wit, 1995). The strategy had six themes, with only one (the last) relating to student recruitment:

1 Internationalising learning, teaching and research.
2 Enhancing the international student experience.
3 Enhancing the international experience of home students.
4 Developing and fostering international partnerships and alliances.
5 Developing staff capability for internationalisation.
6 Effectively recruiting international students.

All six elements of the strategy were to receive equal emphasis in order to develop a shared understanding that it was not the intention simply to seek ever higher numbers of international students. Leeds Metropolitan has around 4,000 international students from 120 source countries and there are no plans to increase significantly the number of students attracted to Leeds.

It is undeniable that there are financial benefits from international student recruitment, but the real impact of international students is of a different order and relates to essential aspects of the educational process. These include:

○ providing alternative perspectives in the classroom
○ encouraging staff to diversify research and teaching interests
○ offering opportunities for engagement in international contexts, for example through working with partner universities
○ remodelling the socio-cultural context
○ assisting the internationalisation of home students.

Global perspectives across the curriculum

It is evident that the mere presence on campus of international students, or tactics which entice certain home students overseas, will be insufficient to develop the global perspectives of the entire student body. Zimitat bemoans an

> overemphasis on isolated, bolt-on initiatives (i.e. staff and student exchanges, study tours, multicultural days) that are not scalable, integrated with other strategies, or likely to sufficiently infuse a curriculum to achieve an educational impact on all graduates. (Zimitat, 2008: 136)

His research on student perceptions of curriculum internationalisation shows the relative failure of domestic students to gain the most from student population diversity either in class or on campus. It also indicates more positive perceptions of the social climate and personal orientations to internationalisation by international students than domestic students.

Leeds Metropolitan sought to develop a flexible, integrated and discipline-focused internationalised curriculum, incorporating global perspectives, to make curriculum access for international students easier while also developing the international and intercultural perspectives of all students and staff. But, as Zimitat argues,

> internationalising curricula is not just about content, it also requires changes in pedagogy to encourage students to develop critical skills to understand forces shaping their discipline and challenge accepted viewpoints... [Our research showed that] preparing students for cross-cultural group work was positively correlated with the development of cross-cultural perspectives. (Zimitat, 2008: 141–2)

Leeds Metropolitan's strategic approach (reviewed in Jones and Killick, 2007) saw the development of a framework document to identify and promote cross-cultural capability and global perspectives across the curriculum. Course teams were asked to use the document to review courses in their own subjects, with the help of a series of enabling questions. The document offers examples to assist interpretation and to support staff development for those with limited experience of internationalisation. At the end of the document, suggestions from the pan-university teacher-fellows' network offer help on implementing the ideas in specific classroom environments or subject fields. By the end of 2008, all programmes will have considered the implication of these guidelines for students and course teams, although we regard this as merely the first attempt and will continue an iterative process of review.

In his outline of ways for an institution to approach internationalising the curriculum, Webb identifies four phases:

1 International students studying alongside home students.
2 Systematic curriculum development for internationalisation.
3 Transnational operations and internationalisation of curriculum.
4 Normalising internationalisation of curriculum:

> turning the ad hoc and uneven efforts of a few enthusiasts into the normal
> expectations and requirements of the organisation.   (Webb, 2005)

To 'normalise' internationalisation, he makes the important point that while

> the development of organisation-wide systems is necessary for this to happen…
> such 'culture change' cannot be effected by university edict alone, but only through
> the creative utilisation of the imagination and agency of those who comprise the
> university.   (Webb, 2005: 117)

Leeds Metropolitan's strategic framework has facilitated such 'normalisation' by enabling subject specialists to determine how their own courses should interpret the guidelines. Leask (2008) argues that:

> an internationalised curriculum will develop and assess specific international
> perspectives (knowledge, skills and attributes) through the inclusion of international
> content and intercultural perspectives on knowledge.

At Leeds Metropolitan, we took the view that those with specialist knowledge of each field would be best placed to incorporate such content. We feel that our contextualised approach within a strategic framework has proved to be a helpful means of initiating and supporting curriculum internationalisation across the university. Programmes reviewed to date can be found in the Assessment, Learning and Teaching (ALT) resource for Leeds Metropolitan staff on the Leeds Metropolitan website.[1]

There is still some way to go before change is fully embedded. We are constantly striving to offer opportunities for students from different countries and cultures to integrate meaningfully, both within the classroom and beyond. Local and international volunteering, along with certain student societies such as the Walking Club, offer opportunities for cross-cultural engagement in a focused context, which helps international students as they may lack confidence in starting and maintaining social conversations (Krause et al, 2005). Opportunities outside the classroom for our diverse student population to engage across cultural boundaries include Leeds Metropolitan events, for example the Carnegie Great Student Run, language and culture fiestas or those held in conjunction with our sporting and cultural partners, such as Leeds Rhinos, Northern Ballet Theatre, Yorkshire County Cricket or the Black Dyke Band.

Our partnership with the International Indian Film Academy, which held its award ceremony in Yorkshire in 2007, offered 150 students the chance to meet the stars while volunteering during the weekend's events, but also to engage with a diverse

1 http://www.leedsmet.ac.uk/ALTre-source/cross_cultural_capability_strategy.htm

range of students in purposeful team-based activity. This year, 100 students will be volunteering in Bangkok as the awards ceremony is held there. Others will be working at the Youth Commonwealth Games to be held in Pune, India. Yet more supported the recent African Athletics Championships, held in Addis Ababa, Ethiopia. Leeds Metropolitan's partnerships are creating great international opportunities for students which are enhancing their world-wide horizons. We need to ensure that their experiences are fed back into the curriculum to benefit other students, and indeed staff.

Embedding internationalisation and changing institutional culture

> If internationalisation is to have a chance of becoming embedded it must have the strong support of the Vice-Chancellor, but this is no guarantee that the academic community will either know about it or be willing to invest their time in making it happen. The university needs to communicate what internationalisation means in practical terms and it may not be enough to rely on high-level visionary statements in the corporate strategy. (Fielden, 2008: 4.24)

Leeds Metropolitan recognised that corporate intent and support at senior levels was necessary but not sufficient to achieve the required culture change. Before the days of blogs, we initiated a relatively simple idea which has both supported and reflected cultural change at Leeds Metropolitan and helped to move the organisation from one which merely recruited international students to one which now embraces world-wide horizons.

In September 2003 we introduced a daily on-line *International Reflection* of exactly 200 words and this has appeared each weekday since then, amounting to well over one thousand testimonies from students, staff and friends of the university.[2] The original intention was to raise awareness of internationalisation and to offer real examples that showed that this went well beyond the recruitment of international students. Yet these daily postings have become much more than a source of information and have helped to bring about change in the institutional culture, while at the same time reflecting change within that culture through their growing sophistication (see Jones, 2007). Several contributors note that engaging in the reflective process, and doing so in a public forum, is fundamental to the broader culture of academia, and it may be for this reason that they have been so enthusiastically embraced. It has been noted that, 'change strategies seem to be successful if they are culturally coherent or aligned with the culture' (Kezar and Ecke, 2002) and this may be one reason for their success.

Reflections may offer thoughts on other cultural perspectives, or of different viewpoints on life as an international student in the UK. Many talk of personal transformation as a result of an international experience or encounter. Others help

2 http://www.leedsmet.ac.uk/internat/reflects/index.htm (*IR*)

to raise awareness of global development issues or the need to understand better other communities and cultures, including the needs of our international students. Some respond to world events, including natural disasters, which may have affected students' families. Support staff offer fascinating insights, including the university's driver who surprised his colleagues by describing a Chinese wedding on Valentine's Day 2008, which turned out to be his own (14 February 2008). We ask colleagues from international partner institutions and other visitors to make contributions. International alumni, students on exchange overseas and incoming exchange students offer alternative perspectives on Leeds Metropolitan.

Many colleagues have said how much they value *International Reflections*, one saying that the best of these 'transport' him to other countries or cultures. The *Reflections* have created a focal point which draws staff, students, partners and competitors to the website each day. The ensuing discussion has, in turn, led to an increase in the quality of reflection produced and illustrates changed mindsets towards internationalisation, as shown by this example:

> I believe that *International Reflections* have made the world a smaller place for me, made me understand diversity and given me the impetus and courage to go beyond boundaries by visiting Mexico last year and later this year Brazil. I could pick ten books on various countries in the world but I am more likely to remember ten 200-word *Reflections*. Thanks to everyone who has contributed.
>
> (*IR*, Brian Bolton, 15 September 2006)

Some other ways in which Leeds Metropolitan has indicated its commitment to embed internationalisation are listed here and two are expanded further in the following sections:

○ Securing Fair Trade status.
○ Ensuring sustainable operations such as recycling and ethical purchasing. This led to Leeds Metropolitan coming top of the 'Greenest University' league table. (http://www.leedsmet.ac.uk/the_news/may07/greenuni.html)
○ Developing the International Centre for Responsible Tourism. (http://www.leedsmet.ac.uk/international.htm)
○ Committing to Globally Responsible Leadership. (http://www.grli.org/)
○ Introducing undergraduate and postgraduate modules in living and working as a global citizen, which can be accessed by all programmes.
○ Introducing free-standing Global Citizen Awards at bronze, silver, gold and platinum levels, which any member of staff or student may undertake to show evidence of their world-wide horizons (http://gca.leedsmet.ac.uk/main/)
○ Developing international volunteering (http://www.leedsmet.ac.uk/cpv/index_internationalvolunteering.htm)
○ Committing to a radical new approach to partnerships in the developing world through Leeds Met Africa. (http://www.leedsmet.ac.uk/internat/region/africa/leedsMetropolitanafrica.htm)

International volunteering

In 2007, the centenary year of our Headingley Campus, Leeds Metropolitan embarked on an ambitious drive to develop the global perspectives of students and staff through community and conservation projects across six continents. Leeds Metropolitan paid 50% of the costs for 148 volunteers to take part in 15 projects in ten countries. This financial support was sufficient to enable many to take part who otherwise could not have afforded to, but also offered an incentive for students to raise their own funds. We supported this fund-raising, offering ideas and sharing good practice. We developed procedures, risk assessments and information packs for each of the projects. We trained team leaders who would be in charge of each group and would liaise with the country partner. Every potential volunteer was interviewed and only those who were considered most likely to make a success of the opportunity were selected.

The projects chosen were, in most cases, developed with existing partners around the world. These were either universities or foundations we were already working to support through fundraising. Some projects were developed from scratch using in-country contacts. Projects included building sustainable tourism trails in Indonesia, providing education, training and support for former leprosy sufferers in India, working with Roma children in Transylvania, supporting a community centre in New York State, helping to develop tourism in South Africa in advance of the 2010 World Cup, supporting conservation projects in Australia and raising aspirations of Brazilian children from the *favelas* through sport.

Returning students and staff talked of their lives being transformed by their experiences. Comments made by students include:

> The experience was so fulfilling and really opened our eyes to new possibilities. It made us realise how fortunate we are and how important it is to make the most of what we have... However impossible something may appear it is important to reach out and grasp opportunities, to make the most of every day and to see how in turn, you can make a difference to the world around you.'
>
> (Katherine Moss and Johnathan Gallagher – Poland, 25 March 2008)

> The South Africa experience has been truly amazing and it is difficult to explain the vast array of emotions. In less than two weeks, I have experienced a sense of personal growth which could not be forged by any other means.
>
> (Zahir Sarvani, 5 October 2007)

Importantly, we also had excellent feedback from project hosts, who commented on the outstanding way our students represented the university. Accompanying staff reflected on the personal growth in evidence during the projects:[3]

> What is abundantly clear is that it is not only the recipient countries that are enriched by such programmes. Staff and students receive an eye-opening cultural

and educational experience that may lead to a lifelong attachment and which can contribute to making a difference in many distinctive ways.   (David Jackson)

Most of the volunteering projects were of only two or three weeks' duration. What has surprised us is that such relatively short periods could produce the intense, life-changing impact which students and staff have described. We intend to build on this, offering additional opportunities in new countries in 2008 but continuing our commitment to those projects which worked so well last year and building sustainable relationships in communities where we can make a difference and on projects which have so enhanced the global perspectives of participants. This can now be seen as a real alternative to one semester or one-year academic exchange programmes or work placements for students who cannot take such a long time out of their studies or away from the UK.

Leeds Met Africa

Over the past two decades Leeds Metropolitan has established a network of partnerships with communities, governments and institutions in Africa. These were largely the result of personal commitment on the part of a few passionate individuals, but there had been no attempt to coordinate these or to secure additional benefit for other activities in developing countries. Nor was it always clear how the benefits of the programmes or lessons learned from our African partners fed back into the curriculum for all our students. To combine our efforts through the creation of an 'umbrella' organisation, Leeds Met Africa was launched in 2006, providing a vehicle for the university's continued commitment to seeking sustainable and effective responses to African development priorities.[4]

By learning from past experience and evaluating outcomes we aim to increase our collective impact in an efficient and effective way. We rapidly found that, through sharing experiences from working in different countries we were able to identify common themes which we could apply to new country contexts and for which funding could be sought. Additional income resulted, engaging more people in delivering programmes and so increasing our experience. The Africa Unit at the Association of Commonwealth Universities conducted a study of our approach as a model of best practice in partnership development in Africa and they will be supporting a major conference hosted at Leeds Metropolitan in 2008, along with the Association of African Universities. ( )

Leeds Met Africa has become an exemplar of our commitment to world-wide horizons as it is clearly not about securing income streams but rather its aims include:
○ Seeking solutions to locally-identified priorities.
○ Enabling the widest range of people to access Leeds Metropolitan courses by

4 http://www.leedsmet.ac.uk/internat/region/africa/leedsMetropolitanafrica.htm
5 http://www.leedsmet.ac.uk/conferences/africa/

offering them in-country, and seeking funding to support their participation.

○ Enabling staff and student exchange and volunteering opportunities between Leeds Metropolitan and African partner institutions.

○ Providing scholarships and bursaries for African students to study in the UK.

○ Raising awareness among staff and students in the UK of development issues in Africa.

○ Valuing what we can learn from our engagement in Africa – as well as what we can offer.

The emphasis placed on this project has helped staff and students grasp the extent of the university's commitment to world-wide horizons and the ethical context in which our internationalisation strategy was framed. We now provide opportunities for Leeds Metropolitan staff and students to make a difference through engagement in capacity building, knowledge-exchange projects and volunteering, or through research and development programmes. In turn, these projects and experiences enrich the intellectual and international dimensions of our university and enhance the global perspectives of our staff and students. Our involvement in Africa has encompassed a wide variety of projects and has sought to be consistent with Millennium Development Goals. Many have focused on the role of education in the alleviation of poverty, in achieving equal opportunities through gender balance and in enabling students from disadvantaged backgrounds to access study programmes. Through Leeds Met Africa we seek to enable increasing numbers of African people to use their talents and abilities more effectively for themselves and for the benefit of their communities.

Some examples of our work in Africa include in-country delivery of the Masters in health promotion in Zambia and The Gambia with students funded by the Commonwealth Scholarships Commission. In Tanzania our MSc in facilities management sees students supported by the same scheme. In Malawi we are assisting in the development of a national qualifications and levels framework for the HE sector and assisting with the regeneration of university curricula to comply with these frameworks. In Tanzania we are training a tertiary task force in institutional development in all 190 technical institutions standards we helped to develop. The International Centre for Responsible Tourism enabled tourism students to undertake their first field trip to The Gambia in 2008 to investigate how tourism can be used to assist in economic development. International student and staff volunteers took part in six projects in three African countries during 2007.

World-wide Horizons 2008–12

Leeds Metropolitan's vision of 'world-wide horizons' has ensured that internationalisation is firmly embedded within the institution and integrated with other corporate strategies, including assessment, learning & teaching and research. It has also influenced the development of Leeds Met ACTs, (Attitude, Character &

Talents), our ground-breaking approach which seeks to 'attract, retain, develop and promote staff with the attitude, character and talents to make a difference' (Leeds Metropolitan, 2008). Having made significant progress since 2003 in changing the internationalisation culture at Leeds Metropolitan, we are now embarking on the next stage. World-wide horizons now represents one distinctive element of a Leeds Metropolitan education and the internationalisation strategy is being revised to take this forward. The strategy will reflect more effectively Leeds Metropolitan's vision and character statement. There will be an explicit emphasis on world-wide horizons, which will form the subtitle of the document. Our commitment to global perspectives and sustainable development will be articulated clearly and a more structured approach to staff development will support the next phase. The six original themes will be incorporated and extended into four new categories which will fully embed internationalisation over the coming years:

1 Curriculum and student experience beyond boundaries.
2 A university of international festivals and partnerships.
3 A globally responsible leadership university.
4 Using talents to the full.

Conclusion

Internationalisation has been described as 'one of the most powerful forces for change in contemporary higher education' (Taylor, 2004). This has certainly been the case at Leeds Metropolitan, where its influence over a relatively short period has been outlined in this chapter. It is undeniable that the income which international students can bring is appealing to universities in the face of scarce resources and global competition. However, Luker contends that seeking to enhance the international student experience to protect income streams in the face of intense competition will only work as an 'integral part of a broader strategy for internationalisation that is not motivated by profit.' (Luker, 2008: 12). This chapter has provided an indication of the breadth of Leeds Metropolitan's 'broader strategy' and some evaluation of our progress to date. Discussions about the revised internationalisation strategy are currently underway and these have been very different in tone and emphasis from those which took place in 2003 when the first strategy was being produced. This is a further indication of the culture change which has taken place and of how views of 'internationalisation' have changed in just five years.

The relatively rapid changes since 2003 have arisen from a combination of the approaches outlined here. Crucial to our success so far has been the capacity to engage with colleagues throughout the institution and to open up opportunities for experiences and debate which support our vision of world-wide horizons. A strategic framework, along with commitment and leadership by senior staff may have been the catalyst, but firing imaginations and offering life-changing experiences for staff and students provides the momentum which we hope will deliver enduring change for staff, students and the university itself.

References

Ellingboe, B. J. (1998) Divisional strategies to internationalise a campus portrait: Results, resistance and recommendations from a case study at US universities. In Mestenhauser, J. A. and Ellingboe, B. J. (eds) *Reforming the higher education curriculum: Internationalising the campus.* Phoenix, AZ: American Council on Education and Oryx Press

Fielden, J (2008) The Practice of Internationalisation: Managing International Activities in UK Universities. London: UK Higher Education International Unit Research Series/1

Jones, E. (2007) International Reflections and Culture Change. In Jones, E. and Brown, S. (eds) (2007a) *Internationalising Higher Education* Oxon: Routledge

Jones, E. and Killick, D. (2007) Internationalisation of the Curriculum. In Jones, E. and Brown, S. (eds) (2007a) *Internationalising Higher Education* Oxon: Routledge

Kezar, A. & Eckel, P. D. (2002) The Effect of *Institucional Cultura* on Change Strategies in Higher Education: Universal principles or culturally responsive concepts? *The Journal of Higher Education* 73 (4) 435–60 The Ohio State University

Knight, J. (2007) Internationalization brings benefits and risks: Survey results. *International Higher Education* 46 (8–9)

Knight, J. & de Wit, H. (1995) Strategies for internationalisation of higher education: historical and conceptual perspectives. In de Wit, H (ed) *Strategies for internationalisation of higher education.* Amsterdam: EAIE

Krause, K., Hartley, R., James, R., and McInnis, C. (2005) *The first year experience in Australian universities: Findings from a decade of national studies.* Melbourne: Centre for the Study of Higher Education, University of Melbourne.

Leask, B. (2008) Internationalisation, Globalisation and Curriculum Innovation. In Reed, A. and Hellsten, M. (eds) *Researching International Pedagogies: Sustainable Practice for Teaching and Learning in Higher Education.* Netherlands: Springer

Leeds Metropolitan (2003) *Cross-Cultural Capability and Global Perspectives: Guidelines for Curriculum Review.* http://www.leedsmet.ac.uk/ALTre-source/35698_NEW_GUIDELINES2_WEB.pdf (Accessed May 2008)

Leeds Metropolitan (2006) *Leeds Metropolitan University, Vision and Character Statement* http://www.leedsmet.ac.uk/the_news/docs/visionandcharacter.pdf (Accessed May 2008)

Leeds Metropolitan (2008) *Leeds Met ACTs: Attitide, Character and Talents* http://www.leedsmet.ac.uk/the_news/docs/acts.pdf (Accessed May 2008)

Luker, P. (2008) The internationalisation of higher education: shifting the paradigm. In Shiel, C. and McKenzie, A. (eds) *The Global University: the role of senior managers.* London: DEA. Also available at http://www.dea.org.uk/publication (Accessed May 2008)

Shiel, C. (2008) Introduction to Shiel, C. and McKenzie, A. (eds) (2008) *The Global University: the role of senior managers.* London: DEA. Also available at http://www.dea.org.uk/publication (Accessed May 2008)

Taylor, J. (2004) Toward a Strategy for Internationalisation: Lessons and Practice from Four Universities. *Journal of Studies in International Education* 8 (2) Summer 2004

Webb, G. (2005) Internationalisation of curriculum: an institutional approach. In Carroll, J and Ryan, J (eds) *Teaching International Students, Improving Learning for All* London: Routledge

Zimitat, C. (2008) Internationalisation of the Undergraduate Curriculum. In Dunn, L. and Wallace, M. (eds) *Teaching in Transnational Higher Education.* London: Routledge

ELSPETH JONES is Professor of the Internationalisation of Higher Education and International Dean at Leeds Metropolitan University. She is responsible for leading the university's internationalisation plans. These include all aspects of the international student experience, from recruitment to alumni relations, internationalisation for home students, and associated staff development. With a background in applied linguistics and teaching English as a foreign language, Elspeth has many years' experience of learning, assessment and cross-cultural issues for students from a wide variety of nationalities and cultural backgrounds. She worked at the British Council in Japan for three years and in Singapore for four years. Her output includes *Internationalising Higher Education* edited with Sally Brown (Routledge, 2007), *Setting the Agenda for Languages in Higher Education* edited with David Head, Mike Kelly and Teresa Tinsley (CILT, 2003) and she is currently editing her next book entitled, *Internationalisation: the Student Voice*. She has delivered many keynote speeches around the world and authored a range of chapters and papers on values-driven internationalisation and world-wide horizons. Elspeth also initiated Leeds Met's *International Reflections* webpage and has edited it for four years.

2

Assessment issues for international students and their teachers

Jude Carroll
Oxford Brookes University

This chapter addresses the assessment issues which arise when teachers and students hold different academic assumptions, expectations and requirements.[1]

Students who travel to a different country in order to study do so with a mix of expectations, generally believing the experience will widen their perspectives and lead to better future opportunities. Most expect the new cultural context will challenge their ability to adapt and have thought ahead about how they will cope with different customs, weather, food and so on. Those who do plan ahead say it helps even if, in the end, things turn out differently from the way they imagined.

It is often a different story for academic cultural differences. Over several decades, Cortazzi and Jin (1997) have published and investigated differences in how teaching and learning is organised around the world. They describe how all people remain 'blind' to their own academic culture as long as they remain within it. They assume the familiar is universal until they encounter surprising and perhaps unacceptable behaviours which the perpetrator themselves regards as unproblematic. For teachers, unwelcome surprises might include students memorising and reproducing lecture notes in exams, postgraduate students waiting to be told what to do next when pursuing a research degree or students submitting essays constructed by cutting and pasting large chunks of others' words without attribution. For students, the unwelcome surprise might be failing an exam which they had tackled in the same way as they always did before coming to the UK.

The focus here is on helping students adapt to UK assessment contexts, though Jones (1999), in a study on participation in seminars involving students from many different nationalities, reminds his readers that inclusion and academic success are dependent on teachers' willingness to adjust and empathise, as well as on students'

---

1 The author gratefully acknowledges the permission to use material from her contribution to L Dunn and M Wallace *Teaching in Transnational education* (New York, Routledge 2008).

willingness to try out new and potentially uncomfortable approaches. The same holds true for assessment. International students and their teachers will need to adjust and adapt. Suggestions on how teachers might do this are drawn from a large body of literature which seeks to make assessment more inclusive for students arriving from a range of academic cultural backgrounds and all of whom are seeking to succeed in UK higher education (for example: Carroll and Ryan, 2005; Jones and Brown, 2007; Sletaugh, 2007). Suggestions about managing plagiarism have been widely published, by me and others (Carroll, 2007) and those pertaining to plagiarism and international students were also recently included in Dunn and Wallace (2008) with reference to the particular needs of teachers in transnational higher education.

Students' assessment experiences before UK higher education

Before coming to the UK, students' experience of assessment will have included some or all of the following:

Students' learning was tested through examinations only

This means many students will never have heard of, let alone experienced, course-work (in its many guises). Oral presentations and/or group projects will be equally mysterious.

To pass exams, students had to show they knew the content of the syllabus

Before coming to the UK, many students were assessed only on a quite detailed syllabus, using questions that were similar to or the same as those which had been used on previous examinations and soliciting answers in the form of a short statement of up to 50 words. Sometimes, students were only required to select the answer from a 'multiple-choice' type list. In other instances, students were required to know virtually everything in a named textbook which accompanied the course.

Most examinations were high-stakes, high-speed tests

Examinations were widely spaced, with sometimes a year or more between attempts. Success of failure was often life-changing, especially as it often meant entry to or exclusion from the next level of education. In many cases, answering questions quickly usually resulted in better test scores as it allowed answering of more questions.

Students were graded using systems very different from the UK format

Almost no-one before coming to the UK will have encountered a 100-point marking scale where a pass is set at 40 or 50 and where the top performance is recognised by a mark which disregards the top 25% of the scale. International students say it often takes a long time to understand how UK marking systems designate good work.

In many tertiary education settings, marks are norm-referenced (that is, marks are adjusted so that the results mirror expected patterns) and are used to rank candidates rather than to reflect an individual's performance against agreed criteria, as is said to happen in the UK (though in truth, the picture is more mixed). Marking systems around the world deal very differently with failure. Some systems, such as those used in Greek universities, allow unlimited retakes to improve grades; others, such as in

Japan, set enormously demanding entry requirements then assume all students will successfully complete their degree programme. In some systems, teachers' performance is judged by students' marks which can lead to teachers being present during examinations, helping and correcting students' answers.

In many tertiary educational settings, daily 'homework' is formatively reviewed in class and in a few, even large assignments attract no marks. For example, Chinese students describe writing a dissertation at the end of their undergraduate studies which requires many months of work and is often up to 15,000 words long, yet the work does not contribute to their final award. Instead, students say they do it because it is required and because they themselves and their teachers see it as a way of deepening students' knowledge.

Adjusting to UK assessment regimes and expectations

Of course, no individual system can be characterised with any or even all of the above statements, nor does the UK assessment context offer only contrasting assessment methods, expectations and behaviours to the ones noted in the previous section. However, taken overall, most incoming students will need to adjust to succeed and that may mean surrendering strategies and approaches that have served them well for many years. Some do this easily but most do not. They may lack the confidence to try new ways of showing their knowledge and may be reluctant to take risks when the consequences of failure are so alarming. Adjustment is slowed for some because of their language capacity, especially towards the beginning of their UK studies. Students with language scores that are sufficiently high to gain entry may nevertheless lack the confidence to summarise what they read and, often, the words to do so. Schmitt (2005) has studied what entry scores actually denote in terms of vocabulary and has found a wide gap between anticipated and real vocabulary use. Language capacity also may slow down and narrow students' reading.

The result is students who may not be able to meet their teachers' expectations and a number who may not understand what those expectations are. Whilst a few international students do use the UK university experience to sit back and enjoy themselves, most put in very long days, perhaps investing ten times as long in assessed tasks compared to their UK colleagues. Even after repeated experiences of 'getting it wrong', students can continue to hope that more effort will see them right. Teachers can help these students by trying to ensure their effort goes towards what is likely to lead to success. The next section suggests one way this can be done.

Being explicit about assessment

Students usually welcome explicit instructions on:

- the length of submissions (and the fact that longer is not better)
- the format (with explanations of what a report, poster or essay might be)
- what the assessment criteria mean and how they are applied

- ○ which aspects are being assessed (especially the percentage of the mark allocated to English-language proficiency)
- ○ which aspects of the assessment brief are compulsory and which are guidance or suggestions.

Because assessment is so central to academic success, it helps if teachers ensure information is conveyed in writing as well as through discussion, explanation or example.

Even a statement that seems explicit such as 'Ensure your essay draws on a wide range of sources to support your argument' assumes tacit, shared knowledge. For example, it assumes the student will know what might constitute 'a wide range' or even what an 'essay' might be. The task assumes the student will pose and defend a particular point of view. Of course, these statements apply to many students, both those who have stayed at home in the UK to study and those who have travelled. The challenge becomes how to help them all and especially those whose previous academic culture was very different, to understand and apply UK assessment conventions.

More detailed explaining is probably unhelpful. Instead, teachers can help students make sense of their advice through practice and feedback. Students will welcome seeing and discussing examples of good and poor work plus opportunities to try out new and unfamiliar skills before being summatively assessed on their use. Peer and self-assessment methods, perhaps in a workshop setting, can be useful ways to explore and clarify assumptions (Price et al, 2000) if the teacher and the students are clear as to the purpose of the workshop. Even so, adapting to teachers' expectations is rarely a smooth process. Often, it is not until the work submitted at the end of the first term is marked very low or a fail that some students realise that their ideas about assessment may not match their teachers', no matter how much effort goes into telling and reminding.

Being explicit about assessment also includes thinking about feedback. Explicit, sensitive feedback acknowledges students' efforts and guides them to a more acceptable performance. Feedback is not helpful if it concentrates on what students have not done ('confusing argument', 'no links') or it implies rather than states what is required: ('Is this your own words?', 'What about the Dearing report?')

Explicit feedback describes the desired behaviour

'Put the main idea first then provide examples of how the idea would work in practice'

'Tell the reader when you move from describing the method to discussing whether it is a good method or not'

'If you are using someone else's words, you must enclose their words in quotation marks to show they are not your own words.'

'You should have referred to the Dearing report because it...'

Since such statements take time to create and since the issues are largely similar across many newly arrived students' work, standard templates may be useful. Also, it is useful (and less time consuming) to confine comments to key points or essential information, especially in the early days, so as not to overwhelm students.

A note about correcting students' English
Non-native speakers of English will take a very long time to become fluent, correct writers – if ever. The best way to help them do so is to encourage them to read. However, in the meantime, you will be reading and marking their coursework and offering feedback. This requires teachers to tread a careful line between leaving the student to assume the work is unproblematic because there are no corrections and leaving novice writers feeling devastated because there are so many. I remember one student who described her returned work as 'looking as if it was bleeding'.

One approach to finding a middle way is to note errors of grammar on the first page or so then tell the student the same errors occur throughout. Or you might select one or two types of errors and underline them when they occur. If a teacher acts as a copy editor and corrects errors, students tend to see that as 'the problem solved' rather than taking ownership for the solution themselves. Of course, the student could use an actual proof-reader on some assignments. Many universities offer proof-reading services and almost all provide additional support for English language development. Your feedback could stress how and why the student should avail themselves of this service. Except in instances where the assessment is testing students' grammatical accuracy, you might suggest the student shows the work to an English speaker who underlines errors needing correction.

Plagiarism is a cultural issue
Students often wonder, 'Why all this worry about doing the referencing? Or 'What's the point of rewriting grammatically correct text in my imperfect English?' or 'Why isn't a bibliography at the end sufficient? – as Ha (2006) asserts is the case in Vietnam.

To respond to such questions, answers need to go beyond explaining how to write an in-text citation or the finer points of Harvard referencing conventions. Useful answers for the UK tertiary context rest on the assumption that students must construct their own understanding rather than remember and reproduce that of others.

> 'Understanding' in Western universities is demonstrated by a student who can use a fact in a new setting or who can analyse a theory by taking it to bits, or who can explain something 'in their own words'.[2]

Plagiarism, therefore, is not an issue of whether or not students have copied but instead, whether or not the work which the student submits as 'their own' displays

---

2 Of course, examples of single-answer questions in UK assessments also are common though suggestions around managing plagiarism such as those at the end of the chapter include encouraging teachers to set other kinds of questions.

the student's own learning. (And it is about copying, too, as the paragraphs below will show.)

Some commentators assert that plagiarism assumes individual ownership of ideas, a notion that is said to date from European Enlightenment and therefore, to be culturally specific. Sutherland-Smith (2008) offers a particularly detailed account of the evolution of 'owned' ideas and copyright. Ideas about individual, named ownership of ideas is usually contrasted with those found in academic settings where sharing, consensus and social good are valued and where the goal of university study is not individual excellence but rather, to shape good citizens (Sillitoe, Webb and Ming Zhang, 2005). Such dualistic views are problematic. A three-year study of international postgraduate students' writing practices, including ethnographic study in three different tertiary settings concluded that any visitor to a Chinese university will see textbooks and published papers with citations and, at least in some Chinese universities, a visitor can talk with students who are well versed in the demands and controversies of plagiarism requirements, both in their own setting and when they travel to study (Timm, personal communication, 2008).

So, students' awareness of what constitutes plagiarism and their understanding of the underlying assumptions and belief which explain its importance will vary widely – again, a statement that is as true of UK students as it is for their international peers. There are now a wide range of guides, on-line tutorials and publications that help students understand what a definition of plagiarism such as 'submitting others' work as your own' might mean. There are also many examples where universities have invested considerable effort into ensuring that all students' work is 'their own'.

International students' plagiarism: a special case?

Despite the universal confusion around what plagiarism means, in most institutions, statistics on cases of plagiarism will invariably show international students appearing in numbers which exceed their overall percentage in the cohort. I have heard colleagues say that international students are especially prone to this form of unacceptable academic practice and especially likely to cheat although the pedagogic literature refutes this interpretation of the statistics (see: Pennycook, 1996; Carroll, 2007, Angelil-Carter, 2000; East, 2005). Instead, international students' over-representation in penalty statistics can be explained as an artefact of detection. Bull et al. (2001) found that three out of four markers used change of language as their primary means of spotting plagiarism. My own experience shows that for many, looking for changes in how the coursework is written is their *only* detection strategy with cut-and-paste writing strategies much easier to identify in those for whom English is an additional language. The same explanation may account for why, when international students use so-called 'ghost writing' sites (i.e. where work is commissioned for a fee), this is also easier to spot.

Another way to explain the high percentage of international students is to agree that indeed, they do copy, referring to the practice as 'patch-writing' (Pecorari, 2005). This term describes the way in which writers rely on and use others' words while they are evolving their own 'voice' in English. Many experts in academic writing see borrowing others' words as a necessary developmental step (Schmitt, 2005). This, too, has implications for detection since international students often import relatively long strings of words from the original whereas 'lifts' by native speakers tend to be shorter (Shi, 2004). Zobel and Hamilton refer to this type of writing practice to explain that why international students were 'a clear majority identified as plagiarists by software' (2002: 24).

Deliberate plagiarism

The reader may be thinking that arguments about detection and patch-writing are not sufficient to explain what one academic describes as the inevitable consequences of admitting international students: a 'plague of plagiarism' (quoted by Baty, 2007). Deliberate plagiarism by international students does undeniably occur and there is evidence to show it is happening more often, albeit from a relatively low base (Nagy, 2006). Nor is it difficult to speculate why this might be the case. International students are investing heavily in a university course and so will have a great deal to lose financially and in terms of self-esteem should they be unsuccessful. Brennan & Durovic (2005) found cheating more likely in those who were studying to gain a qualification.

Another explanation may lie in the growing opportunities for purchasing work through so-called 'ghostwriting' services. Clark (2008) estimates there are 250 such sites specifically aimed at UK students and many say the majority of their 'clients' are non-UK students, though few specify whether users are studying at tertiary level. For example, one site (ukessays.com) issued a press release which claimed that in 2007, approximately 1,600 'international students' purchased essays with 60% said to be return customers.[3] While no one who cares about student learning would regard the 1,600 claimed sales at this one site as acceptable, and while the numbers from all such sites are not known but are likely to run into many thousands of purchases, it is important to keep in mind that the figure represents a small total of the work generated by (potentially) 100,000+ international students. Teachers tend to react very strongly to an instance of deliberate cheating which includes 'ghostwritten' work, perhaps because it is often so blatant and/or the teacher fears that identification of one such implies many more may pass undetected. This strong reaction, too, may encourage the view that international students and plagiarism are causatively linked.

In summary, the evidence points to the conclusion that, in common with all students, most plagiarism by international students arises from misunderstanding of

---

3 The site stresses that essays are for research purposes only though prices are geared to delivery a few days before submission, leaving it unclear how purchased essays could be used in this way.

academic writing conventions and from misusing citation rules when attempting to write from sources and use others' ideas and words. The particular difficulty of operating in a second language makes copying by international students easier to identify and more likely to prompt action because it seems so clear-cut. Nevertheless, the issue of the link between international students and deliberate plagiarism remains a topic of particular concern.

Some international students – and the evidence suggests the number is rising significantly from a relatively small base – deliberately fake rather than make their own assignments. All students will need to know what is expected of them concerning plagiarism, most will need specific teaching of the necessary skills, and international students in particular will need considerable practice before they can acceptably 'do their own work'.

Managing assessment and plagiarism with diverse students

Assessment and its unacceptable expression, plagiarism, can only be managed by combining a range of actions, all of which are harder to achieve when working with students who are also getting to grips with a new assessment regime. Those who have tried to do so recommend the following as useful:

1 Create opportunities for discussion and interaction

Staff and students will need safe contexts in which the concept of plagiarism, its complexity and how the rules are applied in practice, can be discussed. Perhaps this means rethinking the induction session to include this topic or making space in a module to cover what is expected. Students simply cannot grasp what is needed without some degree of experiential learning.

2 Become familiar with students' previous experience and their expectations for current study

Look for real examples of how students have learned to generate work prior to enrolment. Talk with students about how they do assignments in their study and which aspects are especially challenging. Actively try and avoid stereotyping or concluding that students' behaviour in the new setting has the same meaning as it would have in a familiar one. So, for example, students who copy large paragraphs may assume you, the reader, know the source and that reminding you of it would seem presumptuous whereas perhaps a home student doing so might be more motivated by expediency or, as one said recently, 'can't be bothered-ness'.

3 Provide clear and explicit guidance

This could take the form of a bespoke course designed to develop the skills students will need to be successful, such as how to identify reliable sources of support for an argument, acceptable organisation and structure in written work, note-taking, strategic reading, using the passive voice and a host of other skills. Of course, in addition, a student will need to master skills linked to citation such as paraphrasing, summarising, in text citation and how to ensure the reader knows which ideas are the student's and which are attributed to other authorities. It is probably most effective to teach academic skills as an integral part of the course, tied to the content and tailored to the needs of a particular discipline or context.

4 Teach the skills you value rather then telling students what they must avoid; adhere to appropriate standards

Negative admonitions ('Don't quote verbatim') are little help to a novice whereas examples of good work (and do offer several lest students think this constitutes a model answer) will be helpful, as will pointers on where to find more information. Ensure your feedback stresses the things that matter rather than, for example, being deflected by comment on the finer points of using the Harvard referencing system.

5 Design assessments which discourage copying

Suggestions include changing the task, avoiding tasks that ask students to discuss or describe (rather than higher order verbs such as 'rank', 'choose', 'justify' or 'evaluate'), asking students to show how they went about doing the work through submitting drafts and even rough notes, and using assessments that authenticate work such as asking students to write about their coursework under observed conditions.

6 Visibly monitor and detect plagiarism

This need not be too time-consuming. You might ask students for evidence prior to submission that they were active or require evidence of process with their submission such as drafts or photocopies of significant sources. So-called detection software such as Turnitin is useful and can be used by students prior to submission (with your control) to ensure sources are cited (Davis, 2007). Even an Advanced Google search will usually unearth the source unless the student has tried hard to conceal it.

Students need to know and see evidence that you are actively protecting academic regulations and values. If you only do this and not all the other measures described here, students may feel they are being watched and treated as cheaters. If you do it as part of an overall package for dealing with student plagiarism, detection will augment and strengthen other measures.

7 Use penalties and feedback carefully

Ensure you distinguish in your feedback and penalty decisions between plagiarism that arises from misunderstanding and misapplication of academic conventions and that which arises from misconduct and which is unacceptable regardless of where and when it occurs. So, for example, a student in the early stages of their UK learning career can be assumed to know that submitting an assignment that is 90% copied from something written by a cousin is not acceptable. Study after study in a range of academic contexts show that students understand this to be the case (for example: Graham and Leung, 2006; Handa and Power, 2005) and when this happens, it should be dealt with in a way that reflects the seriousness of the breach. On the other hand, the same student who constructs a piece of work that is 90% assembled from ten sources (all listed in the bibliography) to create a more or less coherent whole has plagiarised if he or she has not marked explicitly which words are copied and named the source of those words in the text. However, it may indeed be fair to assume that the student believes the patched-together result meets the requirement for 'original work'. Depending on their UK experience, their belief may mean that they assign the breach to 'misunderstanding' rather than 'misconduct'.

A final word

This is a chapter about assessment but as so often happens, also includes much about the problems, deficiencies and misdirected efforts of international students. Many object very strongly indeed to these characterisations of the issues (see Caruana and Spurling, 2007) and challenge the frequent tendency, perhaps also shown here, to place a negative focus on difficulties and deficits at the centre of the discussion. I acknowledge the danger and have tried to refer to difference rather than deficit. In addition, all the points made in the context of international students apply equally to all students in higher education although most home students will not face as wide a range of challenges as many international students.

Tackling assessments in a new academic context, with unfamiliar academic skills that are still developing, in a new language, and where the consequences for failure are so high – this combination of challenges will mean that international students in particular will probably struggle to do themselves justice. In consequence, their teachers and the higher education institutions which recruited and accepted them will need to adapt and adjust in order to support and guide students – all students – through their transition to HE study. If and when they do, all students will have the chance to arrive, survive and perhaps even thrive in tertiary education. Where this adjustment and support is not there, many will still do so.

References

Angélil-Carter, S. (2000) *Stolen language? Plagiarism in writing.* Harlow: Longman

Baty, P. (2007) Immature students without basic English skills enrage Uclan staff. *Times Higher Education Supplement* 30 March 2007

Brennan, L. & Durovic, J. (2005) Plagiarism' and the Confucian Heritage Culture (CHC) student. In *Educational Integrity: values for teaching, learning and research,* 2nd Asia-Pacific Educational Integrity Conference, University of Newcastle, 2–3 December 2005

Bull, J., Collins, C., Coughlin, E., and Sharpe, D. (2001) *Technical review of plagiarism detection software report.* Report available at http://www.jiscpas.ac.uk/docs/jisc/luton.pdf

Carroll, J. and Ryan, J. (2005) Teaching *International students: improving learning for all.* London: Routledge

Carroll, J. (2007) *A handbook for deterring plagiarism in higher education.* Oxford: Oxford Centre for Staff and Learning Development

Caruana, V. & Spurling, N. (2007) *Internationalisation of UK Higher Education: a review of selected material.* http://www.heacademy.ac.uk/assets/ Accessed May 2008

Clark, R. (2008) List of sites associated with 'contract cheating'. http://www.ics.heacademy.ac.uk/

Cortazzi, M. & Jin, L. (1997) Communication for learning across cultures. In D. McNamara and R. Harris (eds) *Overseas Students in Higher education: Issues on teaching and learning*. London: Routledge

Dunn, L. and Wallace, M. (2008) *Teaching in Transnational education*. New York, Routledge

Ha, P. L. (2006) Plagiarism and overseas students: stereotypes again? *ELT Journal* **60** (1) p 76–78

Handa, N. & Power C. (2005) Land and discover! A case study investigating the cultural context of plagiarism. *Journal of University Teaching and Learning Practice* **2** (3b) pp 64–84 http://www.jiscpas.ac.uk/uploaded_documents/luton.pdf

Jones, E. & Brown, S. (2007) *Internationalising Higher Education: Enhancing Learning, Teaching and Curriculum*. London: Routledge

Jones, J. (1999), From Silence to Talk: Cross-Cultural Ideas on Students' Participation in Academic Group Discussion. *English for Specific Purposes* **18** (3) p 243–59

Lahur, A. (2004) Plagiarism among Asian Students at an Australian University Offshore Campus: is it a cultural issue? In Sheehy, F. and Stauble, B. (eds) *Transforming knowledge into wisdom: holistic approaches to teaching and learning:* proceedings of the 2004 Annual International Conference of the Higher Education Research and Development Society of Australasia. Milperra NSW: HERDSA

McGowan, U. (2005) Does educational integrity mean teaching students NOT to 'use their own words'? *International Journal for Educational Integrity* **1** (1)

Nagy J. (2006) Adapting to market changes: issues of plagiarism, cheating and strategies for cohort customisation. *Studies in Learning, Evaluation, Innovation and Development* **3** (2) p 37–47

Pecorari, D. (2003) Good and original: Plagiarism and patchwriting in academic second-language writing. *Journal of Second Language Writing* **12** p 317–45

Pennycook, A. (1996) Borrowing others' words: Text, ownership, memory and plagiarism. *TESOL Quarterly* **30** p 201–30

Schmitt, D. (2005) Writing in the international classroom. In Carroll, J. and Ryan, J. (eds) *Teaching International Students: Improving Learning for All*. London: Routledge p 63–75

Shi, L. (2004). Textual borrowing in second-language writing. *Written Communication* **21** p 171–200

Sillitoe, J., Webb, J. & Ming Zhang, C. (2005) Postgraduate research: the benefits for institutions, supervisors and students of working across and between cultures. In Carroll, J. & Ryan, J. (eds.) *Teaching International Students: Improving Learning for All*. London: Routledge p 130–36

Sletaugh, G. (2007) *Teaching Abroad: International Education and the Cross-cultural Classroom*. Hong Kong: Hong Kong University Press

Sutherland-Smith, W. (2008) *Plagiarism, the Internet and student learning: Improving academic integrity*. New York: Routledge/Falmer

JUDE CARROLL works at Oxford Brookes University as an educational developer and is Deputy Director of the Assessment Standards Knowledge Exchange (ASKe), a Centre for Excellence in Teaching and Learning at Brookes. She was until recently the course leader for the postgraduate certificate in teaching in higher education. As an educational developer, Jude's interests in teaching and learning have focused on deterring student plagiarism and effective teaching strategies for international students. She conducts research, manages others' research projects, writes and lectures widely. Jude holds an MA in adult and post-compulsory learning, writes widely about her areas of interest and is a member of the HE Academy.

3

Strategies for internationalisation
Supporting students through
overseas collaborative partnerships

Sandie Randall
Queen Margaret University

How can partnerships with institutions in different
environments and cultures be made to work to the benefit of
all the students and their experience of higher education?

The strategy for internationalisation in the School of Business and Enterprise at
Queen Margaret University (QMU) is based upon collaborative partnerships with
selected overseas institutions. This develops a supported community of international
learners, whether studying in their own country or in Edinburgh (QMU, 2008a;
2006).

Our experience has demonstrated that the development of international collaborations is challenging. They require careful discussion involving both institutions
before entering into the arrangement, a clear understanding of what and how this
is to be achieved and an agreed process for resolving problems that arise. Delivery
of successful collaborations depends on adequate support by both parties in terms
of staffing, technical support, teaching materials and comprehensive guidance.
Communication channels must be clearly defined. Regulatory frameworks and practice must be embedded to assure and enhance the quality and consistency of delivery
at every institution (QMU, 2008c). Special attention is essential to address the problems that might arise for international students studying in the UK.

We have seen that the benefits of successful collaborative developments accrue to
students and staff of both partners involved, contribute to the internationalisation
agenda and crucially, inform practice in a wider arena. At QMU, internationalisation is defined as the process of integrating an international dimension into the core
of the University's activities, to equip students for careers in multicultural and global
societies and to facilitate widening access to and internationalisation of QMU's educational programmes and research. (Kerley, 2007; QMU, 2006; 2007a; 2008).

Objectives

The key objectives of our strategy for international academic collaborations are as follows:

o To develop sustainable growth in student numbers.

o To widen access to our degree programmes to develop an international community of learners.

o To facilitate the internationalisation of educational programmes and disseminate higher education practice internationally.

o To offer collaborative programmes that lead to the award of a QMU degree
 – where the academic standards and quality of such programmes are equivalent to those for degrees awarded solely by QMU – but in a supportive environment and at an affordable cost.

o To develop employable graduates at home and abroad who are global citizens and who will contribute to a global community.

Rationale

The School of Business Enterprise and Management (BEM) at QMU has recognised the benefits of international academic collaboration as a mechanism for sustainable long-term development and viability within the challenges of the HE environment. For this reason, the school's approach to expansion has been to develop an internationalisation policy based around overseas collaboration that would allow the school to develop a range of international partners whose work and values match those of the school, bringing benefits to staff and students of both partners (BEM, 2007b; QMU, 2008c).

The benefits of partnerships with international organisations support the school's strategy in a number of ways. The approach facilitates the internationalisation of the school's educational programmes: to develop graduates who can appreciate the importance of multicultural diversity, can demonstrate an awareness of the implications of decisions for international as well as local communities and who are global citizens who will contribute to a global society (BEM, 2007b). It also supports the university's agenda to develop a community of learners via widening access by delivering our degree programmes in partnership with institutions overseas (CAP, 2006; BEM, 2007a).

Moreover, with the resources of both QMU and partner institutions, we can offer a UK degree within a supportive environment to international students studying in their own country and at a lower cost than would be possible for an international student coming to study in the UK. The strength of these relationships is that it allows students from our partners to choose, if they wish, to complete their studies at QMU in Scotland, and to do so confidently because they are supported and reassured by the close relationship of their home and QMU institutions. In addition, and importantly, our internationalisation strategy strives to be sensitive in its approach and content to allow us to share higher education practice internationally to add value to the educational resources and intellectual capital of QMU and overseas institutions (QMU, 2008c).

Context

At the start of the QMU internationalisation strategy, India was identified as a country with great potential for the development of higher education and it is in India that the first QMU and BEM overseas collaboration developed. The school has subsequently expanded and deepened its partnerships, both jointly with this original partner and with new partnerships in India, as well as elsewhere.

The degree programmes involved in overseas delivery to date include International Hospitality management, Hospitality and tourism management, and Business management at undergraduate level, and the MBA in Hospitality management at masters level. The number of students studying overseas by franchise at our partner institutions is significant and increasing annually with new partnerships

Description

The collaboration between QMU and its overseas partners is based upon an articulation agreement and the details are set out in a memorandum of understanding (QMU, 2008c). In these agreements, students are admitted to Year 3 of the QMU degree programme within the Scottish Credit Qualification Framework (SCQF) on the basis of an approved prior learning (APL) mapped equivalence of 240 Scotcat credits for successful achievement of the two year diploma undertaken by students at our partner institutions (SCQF, 2008; QMU, 2008b). This articulation agreement offers students the choice of taking the QMU degree either in their own country at the home institution by franchised delivery, or at QMU in Edinburgh.

Evaluation and discussion

This case study examines and reflects on the School of BEM's experience with our partners in India over the last 10 years, where Indian students have studied the QMU degree in International hospitality management at their home institution in India and at QMU in Edinburgh. International collaborations are not without their challenges which should not be underestimated. They require strategic development and investment, operational coherence, reciprocal commitment, clear communication channels and dedicated effort and resources. Notwithstanding these challenges, in our experience collaborative developments enhance the experience of students and staff of both partners involved and, crucially, inform good practice in a wider arena. We are engaged in a process and the purpose of this case study is to share some of the lessons and insights learned so far.

Planning and resources

One of the most important lessons learned has been the danger of underestimating the requirement for strategic planning, strong management and adequate resource investment, particularly at the start, for successful long-term and sustainable collaborations. This requirement has led to the appointment of a dedicated vice principal, which demonstrates institutional commitment, but importantly, the operational management role is delegated to the schools as we strive to embed internationalisation in everything that we do (Fielden, 2007; BEM, 2007a; 2007b). The requirements of an international collaboration must be set out in a memorandum of understanding, identifying the respective expectations and responsibilities of each partner. Important aspects of the agreement are the issues of the frequency, duration and financial responsibility for travel and accommodation costs for staff visits in both directions (QMU, 2008c).

That said, it cannot be assumed from a memorandum of understanding that there is a common view of what is required in an academic partnership, and this is vital for success. Issues that are particularly relevant are quality assurance and enhancement within different educational, business and cultural environments (CAP, 2006; QMU, 2008d). To achieve this common view, intensive collaborative work is required before the start, as well as during the operation of the programme. Our experience has shown that this planning and development is so much more effective if it takes place face to face rather than mediated at a distance. An early investment of time and resources is essential. This reduces the inevitable problems and misunderstandings that lead to failure and lost reputation, while fostering high levels of confidence and trust between the partners early in the relationship to accelerate a positive cycle of sustainable development and success.

A collaborative approach dependent on trust involves some risk, as both sides are equally dependent upon each other for the quality of the project. The choice of partner is therefore crucial. Successful partners have been those whose work is complementary to and whose values match those of QMU (2008c). It has become clear that much of the success of the collaborative work undertaken by the School has been due to the commitment and determination of our partners to take ownership of these programmes and to meet the demands placed upon them to ensure their success. The positive impact of partners of this calibre cannot be underestimated.

Issues of quality assurance and enhancement are central to the challenge of overseas collaborations. The QMU institutional regulatory framework is very well defined for overseas collaboration to ensure the quality, consistency and enhancement of the student experience wherever they are studying (CAP, 2006; QMU, 2008c; 2008d).

As is so often the case, the significance is in the detail. An essential requirement for the development and management of quality-assured overseas programmes is effective operational processes and clear communication channels and, of course, they are interdependent. To address this, the overall management of the overseas collaborations in the school has been consolidated in the duties of the Academic Director (Collaborations and Partnerships), a dedicated management role. This appointment demonstrates the importance attached to these projects. Reporting directly to the dean, the academic director is responsible for developing and managing partnerships, ensuring consistency of policy and quality of practice across the school's collaborations, coordinating the integration of international students into the school and managing the coordination required to maintain such partnerships effectively with our partners, within the school and across QMU.

The protocol for communication between the school and the partners is clearly defined in the *Academic Agreements Handbook* (QMU 2007a). The academic director liaises directly with programme leaders at each partner institution as they are responsible for the operational management of all aspects of the delivery of the programme. For the day-to-day operational matters at QMU, the academic director is supported by two dedicated school academic staff: the school collaborations' coordinator and the international student tutor. The school collaborations' coordinator liaises with staff at our partners and QMU on the practical issues for the delivery of the programme overseas. The international tutor supports the international student experience at QMU. We have recognised the risk of misunderstanding if there is any ambiguity about channels of communication and, for this reason, all communication is directed through or copied to the academic director. The management of the programme and its quality assurance is thus seen to be a shared responsibility with our partners, but with the clearly defined key coordinating function located at QMU.

Enhancing the student experience

Ensuring the quality and equivalence of the student experience across global campuses can be challenging and here we can do most to add value to the student experience. QMU module coordinators communicate directly with partner-module staff on the content and learning experiences of their module in person, via the WebCT site and by frequent and regular email dialogue. When the module is finalised, QMU module coordinators provide each module tutor with a comprehensive teaching and assessment pack. All partners have access to QMU electronic learning platforms, electronic library resources and IT facilities. Our partner staff have full access to the QMU WebCT site for each module, and a parallel site is set up for their own use with their students at each institution. Our ambition is to move to a single WebCT site for all students studying each module to support a virtual international community of learners. However, it should be noted that these developments can be technically challenging across sites, and success is entirely dependent upon continuous dialogue between the academic, support and technical staff at both QMU and the partner institutions.

The heart of the student experience takes place at the level of the module. The relationship between the module tutors at QMU and our partners is therefore crucial. For this reason, a positive and proactive relationship from the beginning is required to encourage regular communication exchanges and full engagement from both partners, so that queries and problems are quickly resolved and the possibility for high quality collaboration is enhanced. This relationship is facilitated via WebCT and email, but one important mechanism is the week-long visit made by QMU module coordinators to each partner institution at the start of a new collaboration programme and then at each subsequent semester. Based around the comprehensive study pack, QMU module coordinators deliver a week's teaching with partner students and module staff, and develop and share understanding of the contents, processes, learning experiences and assessment criteria of the module. These meetings by module tutors have proved to be a crucial element in establishing a firm interpersonal foundation for continuing high levels of engagement.

An issue that has implications for successful UK degree study is that of good scholarship in the context of the differences in the traditions of international students' educational cultures, experiences and expectations. For successful study at QMU, students must be empowered to engage fully in the student-centred, enquiry-based learning approaches on offer (CAP, 2006; BEM, 2007). We enhance the opportunities to deal with this in each collaboration. This allows staff in different institutions to share and understand a range of pedagogical philosophies and practice as a basis from which to work together to address the issue with consistency both at the home institution and at QMU.

We have found the issue of good scholarship skills is linked to the importance of student preparedness for degree study. With our partners, we have introduced and honed a number of initiatives to prepare and support students. These begin in the early years of the diploma curriculum where our partners now embed academic and graduate skills development, address the concept of plagiarism, and offer a wider range of interactive and enquiry-based learning approaches. They are further developed in Year 2 at each partner institution, where QMU staff deliver a one-week familiarisation and transition programme to all Year 2 students and, by the partners, at the start of their new academic year with a six-week transition programme.

For the students who are to study at QMU, where the learning curve is steeper and must be accomplished quickly, the QMU in-country transition programme prior to departure for Edinburgh is particularly helpful. This programme offers an opportunity to learn about Edinburgh life and culture, to become familiar with QMU academic approaches and electronic learning platforms, to resolve relevant practical questions and, crucially, to get to know some friendly staff, in advance of their arrival at QMU. Although this development is relatively recent, early indications suggest the impact of the programme speeds up the transition experience for students on arrival at QMU and leads to some increased engagement and improvement in performance.

For the students choosing to study at QMU, practical arrangements are co-ordinated between the partners to ensure a smooth and welcoming arrival to QMU. A further transition programme is delivered at the start of each academic year at QMU, led by the dedicated international tutor. This programme also includes engagement with the international office for practical issues such as work permits and banking arrangements, student-support services including English language support and a dedicated job fair attended by local hospitality businesses. Following this, all direct entrant students to Year 3 of the programme are offered a module in *Continuing Development Studies* which further develops and hones a range of academic, professional and personal skills, offering students a fast-track route to engagement in the degree programme, to support and encourage fulfilment of their potential. Additionally, the international tutor provides academic and pastoral support to these students throughout the year.

These transition programmes also allow us to tackle at an early point one of the most challenging difficulties for overseas students studying in Edinburgh, that of the temptation to work at the expense of study. This issue poses one of the most intractable dilemmas for both students and for those institutions promoting overseas study. For many of the students, the responsibility of the loans taken by parents to fund their studies, coupled with the temptation of earning what appear to be very large salaries, can lead some students to neglect their studies for paid work. This situation can lead to poor attendance, attempts to improve academic performance through plagiarism and potential failure, with the associated very serious consequences at home. QMU and our partners recognise the problem and attempt at every opportunity to counsel and guide the students. Recently, after much debate, the School has adopted an attendance policy for all interactive classes and this has shown a marked general improvement in performance. It is noteworthy that there are few sources of financial support available for international students; there is one bursary available to these students sponsored by a member of staff. This is an issue that merits attention for the future if we are to support widening access internationally.

Interestingly, results emerging from the first-year experience enhancement theme suggest that the extent to which the student becomes academically and socially connected with the institution can be an influence on student empowerment and engagement (Gordon, 2008). A bonus of the collaborative partnership approach is that student familiarisation with QMU begins early and is not restricted to formal transition and teaching programmes. All QMU visits to our partner institutions involve meetings with the students in Years 1 and 2 who will be potential QMU students in later years, as well as the current Year 3 students. In addition, a member of QMU staff annually participates in the recruitment process to Year 1 of our partners' diploma programmes at a number of large recruitment events throughout India. This is an opportunity to inform the partner's approach to student selection for degree study and to develop a relationship with these students from the earliest stage of their academic career with QMU.

Quality enhancement and staff development

Our experience suggests that successful international study depends upon a close and collaborative relationship coupled with a quality-enhanced approach (QMU, 2008a; 2008c; 2008d). One implication of this is our responsibility to support our partners in ways that allow them to participate fully in the relationship from an informed position and this requires appropriate staff development.

The academic director works closely with the team from the beginning of developing a new relationship. Before the start of programme delivery, the director of QMU's Centre for Academic Practice (CAP) and the academic director deliver a staff development programme at the partner institution, to develop a shared understanding of QMU academic standards and processes. Annually, CAP deliver staff development workshops in each partner institution, or when possible, jointly at a selected institution overseas. The academic director is in continuous contact with each institution and makes regular visits.

Staff from all our partners visit QMU annually to engage in activities in the school and university. In this way, the reciprocal sharing of ideas and practice fosters a higher level of understanding in a multicultural environment. The professional and social aspects of these visits foster good interpersonal relationships between partner staff and we have found that these personal relationships are the cement and strength of collaborative partnerships. All partner institutions conduct regular staff development programmes, and the staff responsible for these maintain a dialogue with their counterparts in CAP at QMU. We encourage and support our partners to pursue Masters or PhD programmes at QMU, and it is our shared ambition shortly to embed longer periods of staff exchange.

Internationalising the curriculum and developing an international community of learners

The collaborative partnership approach has enabled us increasingly to internationalise the curriculum and to widen access with sustainable international student numbers overseas and at QMU.

Although our collaborations are based on franchised delivery of our QMU programmes, our approach to curriculum development has been to develop the programme collaboratively in partnership. At the time of programme validation and/or review at QMU, and for the annual review of each module and assessment, QMU module leaders engage with their counterparts overseas to develop a curriculum and learning approach that is informed by cross-cultural and multicultural contexts (BEM, 2007a). The outcomes of this are consolidated in a fully comprehensive teaching pack for every module.

These developments are not limited solely to the content of the module. With our partners, we share ideas and approaches to access a widening range of learning and teaching experiences for an increasingly diverse and multicultural student population.

This developing knowledge and practice informs the curriculum and the pedagogy at all sites and the ways in which we manage and develop the learning experience for the international students who choose to study at QMU.

It has been our ambition to offer a student-exchange programme with our partners. Although this has not proved as straightforward as we hoped, as a first step we are now planning study tours of a fortnight or so between QMU and our partners in India for the next academic year. Those students undertaking this trip from QMU will act as mentors to the students coming to study at QMU in the following year. We are also actively working on international placements/work experiences organised through our partners.

We recognise that the transfer of international students to study at QMU is a crucial process. As the relationships have matured, the expansion in student numbers led the school and its partners to a more strategic approach of careful planning and management of the students' transition experience. At QMU, the school appointed a dedicated international tutor to manage and support the international students and their integration, and to develop and hone the transition programmes. This work is enhanced by the presence of the international tutor from one of our partners, who accompanies the students to QMU and works with QMU colleagues for the period of the induction/transition period at the start of the new academic year.

The influx of international students in the school inevitably has an impact on the expectations of the existing cohort of students, and it was recognised that the experience of these students required management. The international tutor works very closely with the QMU programme leader to ensure that both the international students and the existing students are prepared and integrated for the changed student culture at Year 3. Although issues of diversity and cross-cultural awareness are embedded in the curriculum (BEM 2007a), staff take care to prepare the existing students for the new context, and talk through the implications of this. Interestingly, although there have been some limited examples of dissatisfaction from existing students, the majority of students speak very positively about the enriched experience of learning within an international community of learners (Fielden, 2007: 25). However, we do recognise that managing large cohorts of international students does present a potential issue, and this is monitored carefully.

We acknowledge that international students on campus at QMU can present challenges, but they also offer a number of academic benefits. The international students make an important contribution to the cross fertilisation of ideas for a widening curriculum and more varied learning experience for the 21st century world, to the benefit of a wider community of learners. The presence of international students on degree programmes can positively change the nature of the learning culture if harnessed to advantage. Learning experiences are enriched by a range of different cultural mind sets and sensitised to political, economic, philosophic and cultural differences. Debates are informed by multicultural perspectives, international case studies and personal global experiences. Problem-solving is forced to take account of the complexity and interdependence of decision making in a global world and impacts of local decision making are related to the global picture. Staff at QMU have been inspired by the understanding and insights of our partner Indian students. In this way, the student experience at QMU becomes increasingly enriched and global in outlook and practice, to develop graduates who are highly employable and professionally mobile (Fielden, 2007; BEM 2007a).

Conclusion

This case study has attempted to outline and evaluate a number of key issues that have arisen as the School of Business, Enterprise and Management at QMU has embraced internationalisation through collaborative overseas academic partnerships. The experience is probably similar to that of others who are engaged in the internationalisation process, but for the school the key lessons learned have been the importance of:

- Selecting overseas partner institutions who share a commitment to QMU's philosophy and objectives regarding the nature and quality of intended educational activities.
- A comprehensive memorandum of understanding that specifies the objectives, content, and respective obligations of the two partner institutions, including the frequency, duration and financial responsibility for staff visits in both directions.
- Staff development for a shared understanding of what is required of an academic partnership, especially in terms of pedagogy and quality assurance and enhancement processes within different multicultural contexts.
- Proactive and frequent staff contact including visits in both directions, to build up personal relationships, to ensure more effective collaboration.
- Strategic planning and adequate resource investment, especially at the start, by both partners.
- Robust management and co-ordination of operational planning and co-ordination and clear identification of responsibilities and lines of communication at QMU and with partners, to ensure a consistent and high quality student experience.
- The development of a joint curriculum informed by multicultural and global perspectives for an international community of learners.
- Comprehensive programme documentation and module learning resources for a supported and consistent shared programme delivery.
- Student access to electronic learning platforms and resources at all institutions.
- Preparation of all students within a multicultural environment for study on the QMU degree programme.
- Collaborative preparation and co-ordination for students transferring to study in Edinburgh.

○ Dedicated staff and resources for managing and supporting induction of international students at QMU.
○ Engagement and preparation of current students at QMU for changes involved by arrival of new international students.

Our experience of the process has been very positive for all partners and their students. The success enjoyed to date reflects the shared commitment, mutual trust and respect that have allowed us to work as a team, resilient and strong in our shared ownership, to address jointly the difficulties that inevitably are encountered.

References

BEM (2007a) *Review of Undergraduate Degree Programmes*. Edinburgh: School of Business, Enterprise and Management, Queen Margaret University

BEM (2007b) *School Operational Plan 2007–12*. Available from http://intra-serv.qmuc.ac.uk/ Accessed 10 April 2008

Centre for Academic Practice (2006) *The Quality Enhancement of Learning teaching and Assessment Strategy*. Available from: http://www.qmu.ac.uk/ Accessed 6 April 2008

Fielden, J (2007) *Global Horizons for Universities*. London: The Council for Industry and Higher Education

Gordon, G. (2008) The Nature and Purposes of the First Year: Sharing and Reflecting upon Experiences and Initiatives in *The First Year Experience, Enhancement Theme*. Glasgow: University of Strathclyde, Centre for Academic Practice and Learning Enhancement

Kerley, R. (2007) *QMU Internationalisation Strategy*. Edinburgh: Queen Margaret University. Available from http://intra-serv/sites/sppu1/ Accessed 10 April 2008

QMU (2007a) *Academic Agreements Handbook*. Edinburgh: Queen Margaret University. Available from http://www.qmu.ac.uk/quality/documents/ Accessed 16 June 2008

QMU (2007b) *QMU Strategic Plan 2007–12*. Edinburgh: Queen Margaret University. Available from: http://intra-serv.qmu.ac.uk/sites/sppu1 Accessed 10 April 2008

QMU (2008a) *Collaborative Partnerships* Edinburgh: Queen Margaret University. Available online at: http://www.qmu.ac.uk/the_university/partnerships.htm Accessed 16 June 2008

QMU (2008b) *Recognition of Prior Learning*. Edinburgh: Queen Margaret University. Available from http://www.qmu.ac.uk/quality/documents/ Accessed 16 June 2008

QMU (2008c) *QMU Policy on Academic Collaborations*. Edinburgh: Queen Margaret University. Available from http://www.qmu.ac.uk/quality/documents/ Accessed 16 June 2008

QMU (2008d) *Quality Assurance Handbook* (On line) Edinburgh: Queen Margaret University Available from http://www.qmu.ac.uk/quality/qa/default.htm. Accessed 16 June 2008

Scottish Credit and Qualification Framework (2008) *Level Descriptors* (On line) Available from http://www.scqf.org.uk/AbouttheFramework/LevelDescriptors.aspx? Accessed 16 June 2008

SANDIE RANDALL is currently the Academic Director (Collaborations and Partnerships) in the School of Business, Enterprise and Management at Queen Margaret University, Edinburgh. In this and her previous posts within the School as Head of Subject for Learning and Teaching and for Hospitality Tourism and Leisure, she has managed the development and delivery of the overseas collaborations. She works with the school and its partners in India and elsewhere overseas, and has endeavoured to incrementally develop practice to assure and enhance the quality of the international student experience at QMU and overseas. In collaboration with one Indian partner institution, she has coordinated the preparation for the QAA audit of overseas collaborations in India for the 2008–09 academic session.

4

Assessing the international dimensions of degree programmes

Nina Becket and Maureen Brookes
Oxford Brookes University

What makes a degree programme 'international'? How far do
UK 'international hospitality' degrees live up to this standard,
and do they deliver real cross-cultural competences?

Objectives

This chapter has two key objectives. The first is to provide a framework of internationalisation that can be used to assess internationalisation within individual programmes of study. The second objective is to identify the extent of internationalisation of UK undergraduate international hospitality degree programmes through the application of this framework.

Rationale

There is no disputing that globalisation is a major factor in higher education (HE) today. As knowledge becomes a more critical resource, HE has been recognised as an important medium for cross-border flows of both knowledge and people. HE institutions (HEIs) are charged with the responsibility of producing graduates who are 'global citizens' (Shiel, 2006) capable of operating effectively in the 21st century. To develop these graduate capabilities, internationalisation is placed high on the agenda in many higher education institutions and departments. However, Knight (2004) argues that within HE, internationalisation is interpreted and implemented in different ways in different countries and by different stakeholders. In addition, critics argue that there is often a gap between rhetoric and reality (Ozerdem, 2006) suggesting a need for further research on how to internationalise higher education in order to produce global citizens.

Context

Various environmental forces are driving the internationalisation of HE. The inclusion of education services within the General Agreements on Trade in Services

(GATS) and the development of the European Higher Education Area (EHEA) and the Bologna process have created a demand for degrees to be internationally recognised and to be portable between countries and institutions (Heitmann, 2005). From a socio-cultural perspective, the OECD (2004) reports on a desire to promote mutual understanding across an increasingly diverse and mobile population. The importance of developing cross-cultural understanding and capability is also recognised in an increasingly globalised business economy that 'encourages the development of a market for internationally orientated and qualified graduates' (Elkin, Devjee and Farnsworth, 2005: 318). These graduates are global citizens who also serve to reinforce national economies.

Schecter (1993) suggests that internationalisation goals can be classified as:

○ Pragmatic

Acquisition of skills and knowledge for employability in a global context.

○ Liberal

Developing an appreciation of cultural differences and inter-cultural sensibility.

○ Civic

Developing multidimensional global citizenship.

However, a recent Centre for Higher Education Policy Studies (CHEPS, 2005) report emphasises the economic reasons for internationalisation, particularly within the UK. The authors suggest that economic drivers can be related to improving the international competitiveness of the higher education sector itself, or the international competitiveness of the national economy. For HEIs, Harris (2006) suggests that internationalisation as an indicator of excellence is frequently used as a competitive marketing strategy.

The drivers and goals of internationalisation are important as they underpin how internationalisation is defined by individual HEIs and the subsequent policies and practices implemented (Schoorinan, 1999; Ozerdem, 2006). For example, economic pressures resulting from 'massification' and reduced government funding have required many UK HEIs to seek alternative funding through international student recruitment, international franchise agreements, or the delivery of programmes overseas. Socio-cultural factors, on the other hand, have seen greater emphasis placed on the development of cross-cultural skills in line with Schecter's (1993) liberal goals.

As a result of the different approaches adopted, internationalisation as a construct within HE remains characterised by fuzziness (Kehm and Teichler, 2007). However, there is some consensus that internationalisation is a process (Gacel-Avila, 2005) and therefore Knight's (2002: 3) definition as 'the process of integrating international dimensions into the teaching, research and service functions of higher education institutions' finds favour with many academics.

Knight (2003) further advises that internationalisation as a process consists of two streams, internationalisation at home and internationalisation abroad. The first stream is concerned with helping students develop international understanding and intercultural skills without ever having to leave the campus. The second stream comprises the same activities but requires the movement of people or programmes within international environments. Building on Knight's work, Black (2004) considers both people and learning activities within her international classification as follows:

○ Faculty
  exchange, international joint research and consultancy
○ Students
  exchange, double degree programmes, joint international programmes
○ Curriculum content
  internationalising courses, adding international courses, adding languages, work or study abroad
○ International alliances
  faculty exchange, student exchange, double degree or joint degree programmes.

These factors predominantly reflect the formal elements of programmes, yet the importance of informal elements of the student experience within HE is increasingly recognised. Extracurricular activities at programme or institutional level can help to support the international experience of students. A culturally diverse student body can also impact on the informal internationalisation of the student experience and has been considered a key resource to facilitate the development of an appreciation of cultural differences and intercultural sensibility (Seymour, 2002). International networking and conference participation by faculty members also serves to enhance the internationalisation of programmes of study for these same reasons. These networking opportunities are also possible post graduation through alumni members and services.

A framework for assessment of internationalisation

As the preceding discussion suggests, internationalisation within HEIs is wide-reaching and potentially complex to implement, given the inter-related nature of the different dimensions identified. However, Raftery (2007) draws together these different components to provide a framework with seven key dimensions of internationalisation:

○ internationalisation of the curriculum
○ internationalisation of the student experience
○ international recruitment
○ international partnerships and strategic alliances
○ international exchanges (staff and students)
○ international research
○ alumni relations.

These dimensions can be incorporated into internationalisation strategies at institutional or programme level and include formal and informal elements, people and learning activities as well as internationalisation at home and abroad. In order to use this framework to assess the extent of internationalisation within institutions or

Table 1   A framework of programme internationalisation

Dimensions of internationalisation	Key indicators
Internationalisation of the curriculum (generally reflective of more formal elements)	Programme aims and outcomes Teaching which focuses on the European and global business environments International case studies and learning materials An international perspective in all main functional areas Opportunity to study a foreign language
Internationalisation of the student experience (reflective of both formal and informal elements)	A concern for intercultural exchange in the classroom Opportunity for intercultural exchange in a social or other informal setting The provision of internships or project work across borders The involvement of international visiting professors The recruitment of non-nationals to the faculty The international experience of faculty The foreign language skills of faculty
International recruitment	Recruitment of students from other countries Support provided for international students
International partnerships and strategic alliances	Courses jointly designed and taught with partner schools abroad The involvement of faculty in international networks
International exchanges (staff and student)	Existence of exchange programmes Internships and study abroad as an integral part of programmes Courses taught in English in non-English speaking countries The opportunity for faculty to serve as visiting professors abroad
International research	Participation in international conferences Research and publication of an international nature
Alumni relations	The international placement of graduates The language ability of graduates

(Brookes and Becket, 2008)

programmes, each of these dimensions requires more specific criteria by which to gauge the extent to which the dimension is developed.

Within degree programmes for management and business administration, one of the most comprehensive sets of guidelines for internationalisation has been developed by the European Quality Improvement System (Equis).[1] These guidelines also

1 www.efmd.org

provide key indicators for assessing internationalisation. Table 1 draws together Raftery's (2007) dimensions and Equis key indicators to create a framework for evaluating the internationalisation of degree programmes. In the following section this framework is applied to UK undergraduate international hospitality management degree programmes to assess the international dimensions of current provision.

Internationalisation of UK hospitality management programmes

The hospitality industry has long been characterised as global, and firms across a wide range of industry sectors continue to internationalise at a rapid pace. Hospitality firms are reported to generate US$950bn annually to the global economy and employ over 60 million people (IH&RA, 2008). As such, there is a demand for university graduates who are global citizens capable of working effectively within the industry, and international hospitality management degrees have been developed across the world as a result.

Within the UK the importance of developing hospitality graduates as global citizens is reflected to some extent in the Quality Assurance Agency (QAA) benchmark statement for undergraduate hospitality provision. These benchmark statements are subject specifications used in the UK to inform programme design and quality review. A 2005 study conducted by Lunn (published 2006) as part of a Royal Geographical Society and IBG project on global perspectives investigated UK hospitality and tourism management degree provision, including international programmes. The authors concluded that while the subject areas have the potential to develop strong global perspectives, at that point in time only moderate global perspectives were developed amongst graduates. These findings suggest there might be room for improvement in the internationalisation of these degrees; however, there are limitations to this study as Lunn reviewed only secondary data available in the public domain.

In order to provide a more complete picture of the extent of internationalisation in current UK undergraduate international hospitality management provision, research was undertaken by the authors using the framework developed. The first stage involved a review of publicly available secondary data (as did Lunn's study) but in conjunction with programme specifications. In the second stage, structured telephone interviews were undertaken with 13 programme managers, thereby incorporating 60% of the UK current provision.

Identifying international dimensions

Given the international nature of the hospitality industry, there is enormous scope for the development of global perspectives within curricula in line with the QAA benchmark requirements and the programmes investigated in this study are making concerted efforts to do so. This section provides an overview of the current extent of internationalisation in UK international hospitality management degree programmes presented according to the seven dimensions of the internationalisation framework.

Internationalisation of the curriculum

The development of graduates 'capable' and/or 'prepared for' working in the international/global hospitality industry or international organisations is recognised as a fundamental aim of most programmes. Cross-cultural capabilities are deemed an essential skill required by graduates. Furthermore, cross-cultural competencies are considered necessary at both a business and a personal level. Assessment of these aims is through the mapping of learning outcomes at module level and through assessment that is constructively aligned with these outcomes. However, this could perhaps be addressed more rigorously in some programmes.

Two main approaches are used to develop student perspectives of internationalisation; either through explicitly titled modules or through a fully embedded approach. In the former, modules are frequently more prominent in later stages of study and sometimes these are solely through generic management modules. Finance modules are frequently more difficult to internationalise. In the second approach, internationalisation is fully embedded in a holistic manner within programmes. Internationalisation is embedded through the nature of the discipline being studied, the use of international case studies, the particular context of the modules, by drawing on the international background of students, or by academic staff providing international industry examples. However, sometimes there is a lack of transparency about how global perspectives are explicitly developed.

Languages are considered to be an effective way of creating an international dimension to programmes. The majority of programmes offer the option to study a language and gain credit towards the degree, with one exception where languages are studied in addition to the degree requirements. However, there are often practical issues relating to location and timetabling conflicts that inhibit students taking these modules. These implications are often exacerbated by institutional policies driven by funding requirements.

Internationalisation of the student experience

The contribution of international students to the development of global perspectives is well recognised. Efforts are made to draw effectively on this resource, facilitated by the high percentage of international students attracted to UK hospitality management degrees. It is generally perceived to be important to get students interacting at the start of their programmes and induction activities are often used for this purpose. Almost all programmes use informal social events as part of induction; however, most are optional.

There also appears to be a genuine concern for inter-cultural exchange within the classroom. Cross-cultural work groups within individual modules are generally considered to be a very important formal international dimension of programmes of study. Approaches taken to forming cross-cultural groups vary with some using an ad hoc approach, and relatively few suggesting that this is undertaken on a formal basis to ensure cultural diversity within groups. In one programme however, cross-cultural awareness and skill development is mapped across the programme and forms part of course validation.

The importance of international or shared experiences of both staff and students in developing graduates with cross-cultural skills is well recognised. Throughout programmes cultural experiences are shared by asking students to draw on their own backgrounds and experiences, or by drawing on the international work or academic experiences of staff members. However, this approach requires staff and students to have a mindset open to exploring and embracing different cultural perspectives. A high percentage of international staff and/or staff with international work experience is perceived to enhance the potential for internationalisation through shared experiences.

The use of visiting academics is related to the existence of research centres which predominantly encompass tourism or retail management. It appears that there may be less international research activity in hospitality than in other business subjects.

Internationalisation-learning activities at home are generally well supported in UK degree programmes, although internationalisation abroad activities are more challenging and these are discussed below under international exchanges.

International recruitment

As the preceding section indicates, international recruitment remains a priority for UK international hospitality programmes where the proportion of international students ranges between 10 and 95%. However, there is some difficulty in assessing the percentage of students from outside the UK due to funding models for students from within the EU. In addition to the cross-cultural contribution of these students, their financial contribution is also important. As a result, support for international students is quite extensive with induction programmes up to two weeks long at university, department and programme level. Continuous language and teaching support tends to be offered throughout all programmes at departmental, school or university level. These services are usually in addition to a university level international student office offering administrative and non-academic support services such as visa, financial or housing assistance.

International partnerships and strategic alliances

International recruitment is also reflected in the extent of credit-rating agreements held across a wide range of international institutions. Although international students can enter most programmes at any level of study, the majority join after completing a diploma programme in order to gain a degree qualification. This frequently changes the international constituency of student cohorts in the final year of programmes and enhances the potential for further cross-cultural exchanges at this later stage of study.

The majority of departments are also working collaboratively with partner institutions outside the UK through the franchising of degrees, predominantly with India, Singapore and Europe. While probably driven by economic initiatives, these partnerships provide further scope for staff members and students to engage in international exchanges.

International exchanges

Despite these opportunities, staff and teaching exchanges do not feature highly within the programmes reviewed, although there are Erasmus exchanges being undertaken within Europe and some funding support for these. International study exchanges also appear to be a less attractive option for students according the research undertaken. Educators recognise the potential of these to help achieve programme aims but there is concern over a decrease in student demand due to funding issues and language barriers. Most funding comes from external sources, such as Erasmus or educational trust funds. The increase in the diversity of the student body is also likely to inhibit the uptake of study abroad, as a result of age and personal or family commitments. When hospitality students do undertake study exchange, those offered at programme, rather than university, level are more popular with students. These exchanges tend to be developed through personal networking by individual academics who then frequently became a champion for them.

International placements often suffer from the same complaints. These are not compulsory in the majority of programmes and in one programme a placement is an alternative to international study exchange. Students are actively encouraged to take up the opportunity of an international placement but there are often difficulties related to the financial constraints of students or their demographic backgrounds. An international placement is normally considered to be one outside the student's home country, with one exception where an international company within the UK is deemed to be an international placement opportunity.

Field trips are recognised as a further opportunity for intercultural exchange and optional field trips are offered in over half the programmes, usually within an industrial context. However, there are a number of restrictions experienced when organising international field trips that negatively impact on the number of trips offered or on student uptake. For example, visa restrictions for international students, health and safety requirements and funding constraints serve to curtail these internationalisation abroad activities. International volunteering is seen as a potential solution in facilitating intercultural exchange to overcome these constraints.

International research

International research and consultancy tends to be driven by individuals. The majority of international research activity is undertaken through research centres at departmental or school level, drawing on hospitality academics' expertise as required.

The importance of staff attendance at international conferences and networking is recognised on an individual basis, yet only one programme reported a defined policy for attendance and support. For staff members, participation in international conferences, research and consultancy also appears to be reliant on the initiative and drive of individuals, particularly in the face of dwindling financial resources within individual HEIs. International hospitality conferences are hosted to a lesser extent.

Alumni relations

While the importance of networking with alumni is recognised, formal links tend to be maintained at the university level, and events are often hosted in countries that are key feeder markets. Informally, alumni are used as guest lecturers to assist with student and graduate placements and as in-country advisors for recruitment purposes.

Conclusion

Most programmes reviewed for this study have incorporated all seven internationalisation dimensions within their programmes to some extent, and there are clearly a number of strengths in the internationalisation of UK hospitality undergraduate-degree provision. The importance of the development of students' cross-cultural skills is clearly recognised within programmes, particularly within internationalisation-at-home learning activities. Within the classroom, the very nature of hospitality assures that staff and students have an experience of hospitality to share either from a customer or work-related perspective.

Nevertheless, the extent to which these experiences are shared is dependent on the willingness of students and the ability of individual staff members to facilitate cross-cultural discussions. These tasks are also dependent on the mindset of individual staff and students and the extent to which they embrace a truly global perspective. Other formal international learning activities also appear to rely on initiatives of individual members of staff. There is potential to capitalise on this opportunity through course teams taking a more considered approach to maximising the opportunities for cross-cultural exchange within programmes. In addition, programme teams may also wish to consider how to make the international dimensions of their degrees more explicit

Cross-cultural experiences as internationalisation abroad activities are also recognised as very important in achieving programme aims. However, there appears to be an increased reluctance of students to undertake placements, international or otherwise. This is reflective of a general pattern evident since the late 1990s across UK HE (Little and Harvey, 2006). Although not specific to hospitality, recent research by the Council for Industry in Higher Education on graduate employability determined that 65% of employers felt that overseas work experience would make candidates more employable and one third of employers consider a graduate with any overseas study experience to be more employable (Archer and Davison, 2008). Despite the potential value of these international student experiences, they have been dropped from a number of programmes as compulsory requirements in response to student demand and other external constraints. Competitive pressures on individual programmes of study require them to be more responsive to student, rather than industry, demand.

At the same time, politically driven massification agendas have created more diverse student populations and many students are not in a position to travel overseas easily due to personal or financial constraints. As tuition fees continue to rise, financial constraints are likely to further restrict the number of students who are able to take advantage of these international opportunities. Other external factors identified in this chapter serve to exacerbate this decline and programme teams need to consider how to encourage and support students to undertake internationalisation abroad activities. For some students, volunteering schemes that are financially supported may prove to be a potential solution. Greater engagement with industry partners may be another way to achieve this support for students and to highlight the importance of international work experience on graduate employability.

The research identified that programmes have the requisite international ingredients and are constantly making improvements, but whether students graduate as global citizens is often dependent on the extent to which they engage in the opportunities available to them. Furthermore, there appear to be concerted efforts by staff members to encourage international and cross-cultural experiences for themselves and students. Ironically, the very forces that are driving internationalisation within UK HEIs at present are also serving to hinder the extent to which undergraduate hospitality management programmes are internationalised. Further development in internationalisation abroad activities for students and staff would help to enhance internationalisation of hospitality undergraduate degrees. As educators, it is important that we start to address the identified constraints to ensure that we continue to build on the evident strengths.

The authors would like to acknowledge the co-operation from UK colleagues for their contributions to this research.

References

Archer, W. and Davison, J. (2008) *Graduate Employability the Views of Employers*. London: The Council for Industry in Higher Education

Black, K. (2004) A review of factors which contribute to the internationalisation of a programme of study. *Journal of Hospitality, Leisure, Sport and Tourism Education* 3 (1) pp 5–18

Brookes, M. and Becket, N. (2008) What makes a hospitality degree international? CHME Conference Proceedings, University of Strathclyde, Glasgow May 2008

CHEPS (2005) Update FP5 project on Europeanisation, internationalisation and globalisation (HEIGL). Downloaded 21 June 2007 from http://www.utwente.nl/cheps/documenten/heigloup-dae.doc

Elkin, G., Devjee, F. and Farnsworth, J. (2005) Visualising the "internationalisation" of universities. *International Journal of Education Management* 19 (4) pp 318–29

Gacel-Avila, J. (2005) The internationalisation of higher education: a paradigm for global citizenry *Journal of Studies in International Education* 9 (2) pp 121–36

Harris, S. (2006) Internationalising the university? Downloaded 3 January 2008 from www.philosopy-of-education.org/pdgs/Saturday/Harris.pdf

Heitmann, G. (2005) Challenges of engineering education and curriculum development in the context of the Bologna process. *European Journal of Engineering Education* 30 (4) pp 447–58

IH&RA. (2008) ?? Ref please

Kehm, B. and Teichler, U. (2007) Research on internationalisation in higher education. *Journal of Studies in International Education* 11 (3/4) pp 260–73

Knight, J. (2003*) GATS, Trade and higher education: perspective 2003 – Where are we?* London: The Observatory on borderless higher education

Knight, J. (2004) Internationalisation remodelled: definition, approaches, and rationales. *Journal of Studies in International Education* 8 (1) pp 5–30

Little, B. and Harvey, L. (2006) *Learning Through Work Placements and Beyond*. A report for HECSU and the Higher Education Academy Work Placement and Organisation Forum, July

Lunn, J. (2006) *Global Perspectives in Higher Education Subject Analysis: Tourism and Hospitality*. London: Royal Geographical Society with IBG

OECD (2004) *Internationalisation of higher education*. OECD Observer Policy Brief. Paris: OECD

Ozerdem, O. (2006) Internationalisation: a gap between rhetoric and practice? downloaded 22 Janauary, 2008 from http://www.york.ac.uk./felt/resources/internationalisation/ozerdem.pdf

Raftery, J. (2007) Internationalisation. Unpublished internal document, Oxford Brookes University, 12th April

Schechter, M. (1993) Internationalizing the university and building bridges across disciplines. In T. Cavusgil ed. *Internationalizing Business Education: meeting the challenge*. Lansing, MI: Michigan State University Press pp 129–40

Schoorinan, D. (1999) The pedagogical implications of diverse conceptualisations of internationalisation: a US-based case study. *Journal of Studies in Internationalization* 3 (2) pp 19–46

Seymour, D. (2002) University hospitality education for international management: a case of wasted opportunities? *Journal of Hospitality, Sport, Tourism and Leisure Education* 1 (2) pp 3–13

Sheil, C. (2006) Developing the global citizen. *Academy Exchange* 5 pp 18–20

NINA BECKET is Assistant Director of the HLST Network, responsible for leading the network's academic development work. Her current research interests include the internationalisation of programmes and quality management within in higher education. Nina joined the School of Hotel and Restaurant Management at Oxford Brookes University in 1991 following extensive management experience in the hospitality industry. During her time in the school, Nina worked as undergraduate programme director, conducted research into the accounting and marketing interface, achieved membership of the Chartered Institute of Marketing, and managed a British Council project to develop tourism in Bulgaria.

MAUREEN BROOKES is Senior Lecturer in the Department of Hospitality, Leisure and Tourism Management at Oxford Brookes University. She is also Hospitality Liaison Officer for the HLST network and member of the Council for Hospitality Management Education executive committee. Maureen held a number of hospitality management positions in North America before coming to England as owner/director of a Cotswolds hotel. Since joining the department, Maureen has completed doctoral research on the diverse market-entry strategies of international hotel chains. She has also researched and published on marketing standardisation and centric orientation of international hotel groups and is actively involved in pedagogic research with publications on quality management and internationalisation within higher education. Maureen has undertaken consultancy and bespoke programme development for organisations including Marriott International, Rezidor and Whitbread.

5

Teaching and learning in an environment challenged by cultural diversity

Alan Darricotte and Rod McColl
École Supérieure de Commerce de Rennes

What are the teaching, learning and assessment challenges in an environment which has a culturally very diverse student body and faculty? At the same time, this school is undergoing rapid and fundamental institutional change…

Objective
The objective of this case study is to air the issues which confront the École Supérieure de Commerce de Rennes in relation to cultural diversity: the combining of multi-cultural staff with multi-cultural students. We aim to give an account of the solutions that have thus far been applied – or are to be applied in the future – but it is hoped that it will also encourage debate and a mutual exchange of experiences, views and solutions amongst institutions facing similar challenges. We particularly explore the problems of harmonisation of teaching styles, the pressures introduced by rapid change and by external forces. That said we came away from a recent workshop at South Bank University with the impression that our school has certain unusual characteristics relating to its cultural diversity which may well add other dimensions to the discussion.[1]

Context
Situated in the north-west of France, this relatively small business school has 1,658 students, 50 'permanent' faculty members and 130 adjunct faculty. 'Permanent' in French terms refers to faculty members who have a contract with the school giving them, for example, full social-security coverage. However, it should be noted that in this particular institution these contracts vary between a 'five-day contract' and a 'two-day contract', and that salaries are calculated on a pro-rata basis depending on the number of days the person is contracted to work in the school.

---

1 BMAF Internationalisation Special Interest Group workshop, 6 March 2008. www.heacademy. ac.uk/business

Founded relatively recently in 1990, the school is growing fast, with an extension of almost the same size as the original building already having been built and with plans for a further similarly-sized extension being projected for the very near future. It belongs to the prestigious group of French business schools known as the *grandes écoles*.

The school is licensed by the French ministry of education to deliver undergraduate and postgraduate degrees. Institutional and programme accreditations by the British Open University Validation Services (OUVS) means that British degrees are also delivered (DipHE, BAIB, MAIB and PhD). The dual nationality of our programmes necessitates a process of harmonisation of the French and British educational systems which has become a daily juggling act – for which we have acquired a certain degree of agility.

From the outset the school differentiated itself from other *grandes écoles* by its insistence on an international approach to pedagogy, to the recruitment of students and of faculty members. At present 42 different nations are represented amongst students and 20 amongst faculty members. Except for one or two staff the administration of the school remains profoundly French.

All our masters programmes and our PhD programme are taught in English. Of our undergraduate programmes 60% are taught in English in the first year (mainly French students) and 80% in our second year. It is in the second year that we welcome large numbers of non-French students. And, just to complicate things, it should be noted that students come to us from other institutions for the third and fourth years of their undergraduate programmes (DipHE and BA).

Faculty members can be broadly classified as follows :
○ Adjunct faculty who are predominantly French in origin and outlook, but most of whom speak and teach in English.
○ 'Permanent' faculty who represent 20 different countries of origin who all teach in English and may, or may not, have a knowledge of French.

Following the recent arrival of a new director-general, a significant impetus has been given to both research and to teaching with a number of research professors being recruited – each one from a different cultural background. Whereas in the past the high degree of informal contact between faculty members (and also administrative staff) was sufficient to satisfy the needs of a young developing school, it is now apparent that the sudden arrival of a significant number of new faculty demands more formal means to achieve the current strategic objectives both in general terms and more particularly in respect of pedagogical issues. Resistance to change by established faculty members and bewilderment at the apparent lack of organisation by new recruits have, not surprisingly, raised questions which need answers.

Key issues for the institution

In pedagogical terms three main areas demand attention.

○ Establishing mutually acceptable approaches and practices in terms of teaching, learning and assessment at the school by such a significantly culturally diverse faculty.

○ Ensuring that these approaches are coherent with the tasks to be accomplished as defined by the pedagogical strategy of the school.

○ Ensuring that these approaches enhance the value derived from the cultural diversity within the school rather than reducing it.

We have decided not to treat these issues separately for the simple fact that they are, quite evidently, inter-dependent.

To introduce these issues more specifically it is helpful to know that the institution attempts to alert students to the different approaches to teaching and learning issues in a number of different ways. For example, the following table appears in the student handbook for all programmes – along with further verbal explanations of the

Table 1   Alerting students to different approaches to teaching and learning

	Classical French system	Pure case method (Harvard and Western Ontario)	Classical UK system
System	Competitive examination performance Elitist Cartesian Low failure rates once in school	High failure rates in programme Competitive culture within school	Relatively competitive entrance based on A-level performance
Teacher	A 'font of knowledge' Lectures No course book Distributes handouts Provides a 'correction' Teacher takes responsibility	Encourages participation Animator pushes students to do analysis and find alternative solutions Uses a course book as a base Uses inductive method of learning Forces students to defend solutions	Teacher is an expert Lectures about points which interest him and/or key elements Discussions in tutorials/ small groups Expects students to learn outside of classroom
Student	Takes notes Learns after the lecture Does exercise after class Student follows teacher Student is passive Students expects right answer	Student reads theory and reads case and analyses case (including in a group) before class Student takes responsibility for the process	Student is responsible for own learning Student expected to read around topic Student expected to be knowledgeable Student expected to synthesise theory

implications for their learning experience at the school and the need for adaptation to function in a culturally diverse learning environment.

In addition, student group work is so arranged that members of each group are from as many different cultural backgrounds as possible. Part of the feedback session will include a discussion about the issues arising from functioning together. Age-old, but still highly relevant questions such as, 'What did you learn from this experience?' 'What did you find /difficult/frustrating?' incite students towards greater awareness of the experience and the role it can play in their professional development aiming at a career in an international business environment.

Also, it is worth noting that our teaching sessions conform to normal French practice: they last three hours which many foreign students and new faculty members from other cultural backgrounds often find excessively long.

Striving for harmony in the pedagogical process

Three points which have a decisive influence on the student/teacher experience should be noted here:

○ Students come specifically to the school to live cultural diversity at first hand. It is one of the school's selling points.
○ They usually have a romantic idea of what the experience will be like before actually facing it.
○ They are apt (as are we all) to confuse differences which are truly cultural with those which relate to individual personality differences.

Thus the challenge is to create a coherent pedagogical strategy amongst faculty members without stifling individual style, innovation and spontaneity; and which is centred on student needs but which, at the same time, exploits the unique cultural environment in the school to maximum advantage.

Attempts to deal with this issue are being made by holding workshops along with the creation of a website solely for the use of faculty – both 'permanent' and adjunct. We limit these workshops to four per semester to avoid other commitments that faculty have. Attendance is excellent but only represents approximately half of the 'permanent' faculty members, those who consistently display a high degree of motivation in wishing to develop a common, but not exclusive, approach to pedagogy. The less enthusiastic remain convinced that 'they know best' and they already hold the key to all the challenges they currently meet in the classroom. It is a long process to persuade them to share their wisdom. However, there are signs that progress is being made.

Adjunct faculty present a different challenge. Where only half the 'permanent' faculty enthusiastically back a commitment to pedagogical development in terms of the harmonisation of styles, even fewer adjunct faculty are at all positive towards it. How can one demand the same degree of commitment from them as one does from those 'permanent' staff who are present at the school during working hours? Clearly, the degree of commitment, either freely given or contractually imposed, cannot be the same.

It is hoped that the faculty website will help to remedy this to some degree at least by inducing a feeling of belonging to the academic community of the school and also to ownership of the fruits of its labours.

Suggestions have also been made that adjunct faculty should be paid an attractive hourly rate plus expenses to attend meetings and workshops, but where does one draw the line? If this were implemented as a blanket solution, then the cost alone would be prohibitive in view of the fact that many of our adjunct faculty come from the UK or North America. So, what about taking the number of hours they teach in the school and inviting only those who contribute hours above a certain figure? Again, the cost would be prohibitive. Many of our adjunct faculty who teach a significant number of hours (usually seminar style) come from far away and also have other engagements thus making it almost impossible to find a mutually convenient time to meet up.

Despite the fact that the school has an impressive number of staff and students from culturally different origins, it is still the case that management works on the classical French 'patriarchal' system and the institution's administrative staff are practically all French. One of the ways in which this situation impacts on the pedagogy within the school is that there is an underlying (and perfectly understandable) mistrust of anything not done the French way. This is particularly apparent in our first-year undergraduate programmes where French students encounter non-French faculty for the first time. Typically, a French student will leave such a session feeling that he or she 'hasn't had his money's worth' simply because he has been invited to take part in interactive processes of various kinds. To a French student this approach simply means that the professor doesn't know his subject and is incapable of standing up and delivering what is called a *cours magistral* or a traditional lecture with no room for any exchange whatsoever between the lecturer and the students.

Another difficulty for French students is that they find it difficult to understand that when there is an episode of teacher input they are required to be attentive and silent. Being 'polychronic' themselves it appears to be a draconian measure on the teacher's part to insist on absolute silence even for a short period.

In these cases it does, of course, behove the more experienced members of faculty to advise their colleagues to explain their approach to the students before they attempt to begin their first session with French students. Despite this, it is only in their second year with us that French students really grasp what is expected of them. The reason? It is at this point that French students participate – and are often the minority – in classes peopled by students from other countries who have highly developed interactive skills and a whole panoply of expectations related to the modules they are registered for. Cultural behaviour runs deep.

However, this is only the tip of the iceberg. What of the difficulties of the non-

French student who arrives with all his or her expectations in this multicultural environment?

Even small but significant signals indicate some of the underlying attitudes to professors. Addressing the writer, students will prefix the name of a faculty member with mister, doctor, professor, Alan or even, 'Hey, you!' From your own experience of dealing with foreign students most of you reading this chapter will readily identify the cultural background of the students who use each one of these methods of address. Firstly, the Frenchman then the Eastern European and so on. By the end of their stay most of them will have arrived at 'Alan'. (The 'Hey you!' seems to disappear rather quickly – but that may have something to do with a personal reaction on the part of faculty to this appellation. Again, undoubtedly to do with my mixed cultural origins.)

The styles exemplified in Table 1 are, of course, generalisations. They are also presented verbally during induction processes but informal enquiry indicates that exposure to them makes little impact in preparing the student for what happens in the classroom.

It has been observed that the relationship between teacher and student is also a frequent source of confusion and dissatisfaction. It is a common experience to find North American students who say what they think and tend to regard their professor as a partner in an educational process. Here a quite blatant degree of familiarity may exist between teacher and student. This is sharply contrasted with the French student who regards such familiarity as unwonted and possibly undignified and certainly undeserved. With the passage of time and contact with students from other countries who expect a more open and familiar relationship between student and teacher, these students may become more at ease with this approach. We are all familiar with this phenomenon.

So, what is the effect of such diversity on both faculty and student cultural expectations and values? Confusion? No hard and fast rules have been formulated for the behaviour of either student or teacher. Thus, whether in the classroom or in one-to-one encounters, the success of the relationship depends on the individual personality of each concerned. The naïve illustrations cited in the above paragraphs scratch but the surface. With a high proportion of faculty firmly rooted in their own culture – which is equally true of the student body – the success of teaching and learning depends much more on the personalities involved than it would normally.

It may be felt that this is a socially fragmented faculty and that more effort should be made to 'standardise' attitudes to the pedagogical tasks facing its members. Curiously, there exists a well-founded feeling of solidarity and mutual respect between most faculty members but it is rarely transferred into social contact within or outside the work context. To add to what is, after all, a lack of dialogue between faculty members, each professor leaves work to return to an environment which is essentially reflects his or her own culture of origin. (Most have brought their families to France.) By some it is considered to be a 'refuge' from the challenge of juggling with multiple cultures at work which is demanding, tiring and frustrating with, of course, the odd moment of satisfaction in a job well done!

Faculty members thus experience the same challenges as do students upon whom we impose tasks to be accomplished. Their choice of behaviour does, however, tend to be based more on an instinctive reaction to situations rather than to the type of analysis of intercultural encounters to which we subject our students! Perhaps a part solution may be to submit faculty to the same consciousness-raising exercises?

External influences

Our validation by the OUVS has, over the years, meant that the school has been forced into at least a basic agreement about how assessments should be formulated and delivered. A bid for EQUIS and AACSB accreditations is lending a new impetus to our efforts.

That said, recent benchmarking exercises have highlighted the fact that we are fundamentally very conservative in our assessment approaches and that we are not necessarily evaluating the acquisition of learning objectives in the most efficient way. Continuous assessment consists mostly of an individual or group project with all the difficulties concerning issues of fairness attached to that, and a final written, summative, examination.

Two recent workshops at the school – modelled on similar workshops held in the UK which were attended by a faculty member – have had a very positive effect in inciting a more effective approach to assessing student achievement but, as is to be expected, the more conservative members of the community need more convincing!

The impact of sudden and rapid change

With the arrival of a new director general, radical long-awaited changes have caused an expected series of 'tsunami' at all levels of the organisation. Previously, the institution was decidedly weak in terms of the management's commitment to research despite the fact that the previous research director had launched a successful research strategy with very little support except that of sympathetic and proactive colleagues.

The arrival of the new director-general heralded the advent of several new faculty members from Sweden, Germany, China, Canada, Senegal and elsewhere, most of whom are primarily interested in research, exactly what the school needs. The younger end amongst the new recruits had very little, if any, teaching experience. Of course, faculty commitment to the student learning process diminished at an alarming rate as research workloads were also imposed on inexperienced or 'rusty' researchers and, inevitably, the balance shifted.

To redress this, the associate dean responsible for the pedagogy of the school appointed a senior faculty member with both management and teaching experience within the establishment to encourage and co-ordinate teaching, learning and assessment (TLA) related activities. The TLA co-ordinator has no particular authority but has access to project development committees, programme management and other meetings; and also has a coaching and mentoring role to help with the induction of new teaching staff. The lack of executive authority for this mission was a deliberate choice in the hope that initiatives generated by the co-ordinator's activities would be viewed by colleagues as their input rather than as innovation being imposed from above.

The result is that faculty efforts, performance levels and development are being closely monitored across the board and, where there is a need, the means are generally being put in place to achieve them. This approach has resulted in a significant increase in the degree of faculty commitment to, and interest in, student learning in the last few months. The overall effect is a growth towards a more harmonised approach in terms of teaching styles without in any way impinging upon the essential elements of personality and spontaneity which add a touch of charisma to help keep students awake in our long classroom sessions!

Students are thus being exposed to a richer culturally diverse experience which is beginning to make fuller and more intelligent use of the internal resources and environment of the school.

Concluding remarks

It has doubtless become apparent in this chapter that the school is undergoing a period of fundamental change in terms of its development and that this is involving radical strategic adjustments. Faculty response to this change and the effect it is having on the student learning process is difficult to assess at present and much work is needed here. Feedback from class delegate meetings and course evaluation information indicates a more positive trend. The emphasis in comments from student delegates has shifted from the teaching to the quality of chocolate and biscuits to be had from the slot machines.

French management style imposes itself quite firmly despite the significant non-French presence in both faculty and the student body. This is not to be taken as a negative criticism of the French approach to management which, for those readers who are not familiar with it, appears to be based on the vulgarly (in French) expressed *système D*. This consists of much discussion followed by a summary decision taken by the manager after having 'democratically listened' to those included in the debate. The decision is implemented, then a 'pick up the bits when it all goes wrong and make the best of it' strategy is initiated to correct any malfunctioning.

This may seem a somewhat chaotic approach but it can be surprisingly successful, although its success depends entirely on the goodwill of the participants and their almost blind confidence in the skills of the manager heading the project. 'Patriarchal' is the name some might give to this approach to management. Non-French faculty and students are required to make a quantum leap in cultural terms to be able to function effectively with this approach. Failure on the part of non-French faculty to understand this way of getting things done has resulted in a slowing down of adaptation to new challenges.

Drawing all these threads together, it becomes apparent that there are three underlying issues to which no truly effective solutions have been found.

Firstly, global and integrated communication between faculty (both 'permanent' and adjunct) and management needs to be urgently reviewed, after which effective means of communication need to be created to ensure maximum understanding on issues related to pedagogy in the school. The fact that some faculty members have little or no knowledge of French pre-supposes the need to ensure that all information is made available in both English and French – a costly and time consuming activity which is beyond current resources to deal with in a truly effective way.

Secondly, the question of motivating faculty members to adopt a more open-minded attitude to the changes necessary for the development of the school needs to be addressed in a more proactive fashion. This must also be global in its application and endowed with the means to properly measure the effect of changes already made or those which are to be introduced

Thirdly, if students – and particularly students from different cultural backgrounds – are to enjoy an optimal learning experience at the school, then faculty have to be made more aware of specific student learning difficulties. The question of learning in a second (foreign) language has not been tackled here but it has been shown that it plays a significant role in slowing the learning process down.[2] Likewise, it behoves the school to seriously consider ways in which faculty are made aware of their own difficulties in coping with cultural diversity – in the same manner as students are – so that a greater understanding of, and thus a better adaptation to, the needs of our students is achieved. Clearly, these points are inseparable simply because they are interdependent.

There is, of course, an alternative way of regarding this unique period of development in the school's history. In may well be viewed, and put to use as, a multi-faceted, multi-cultural management learning process which concerns all members of the community: students, faculty and administration. After all, the degree of cultural diversity of those involved is unusually high and the juxtaposition of a multicultural faculty with that of a multicultural student body presents an opportunity not to be missed. This rich field for research is slowly being recognised as such in the school.

Finally, we would welcome comments, ideas, or relevant experiences which might further the development of these issues – expressed in either a formal or informal way.

2 *The International Journal of Human Resource Management* **12** (8) December 2001 p 1292–312

ALAN DARRICOTTE is Head of Marketing at the École Supérieure de Commerce de Rennes, France, where he subsequently became MBA Director. He has recently been appointed co-ordinator of teaching, learning and assessment activities within the school with a special brief to develop these aspects in the context of the cultural diversity of the school.

He has a worldwide experience in business, teaching and coaching. His first appointment, in the after-sales service of Pennwalt Engineering Inc, for which part of the brief was to teach existing staff the principles of marketing, awakened an early interest in teaching and learning. Following this, various posts along with much consultancy work led to requests from companies to prepare their employees for overseas missions.

Since 1989 Alan has taught in various universities which have an interest in advancing their pedagogy in an international context.

ROD McCOLL is a Professor in Marketing at ESC Rennes School of Business. He has more than 25 years academic experience in Australia, Asia and France. Dr McColl has a doctorate in education, a master's degree in business (research) and a bachelor's degree in marketing. Over the past 15 years he has also completed more than 300 marketing studies across many countries.

Rod is a co-author of *Marketing in Australia* 2nd ed, Australia's largest selling marketing text and is lead author of *Services Marketing: A Managerial Perspective* published by McGraw-Hill. Recent peer reviewed articles have appeared in the *Journal of Customer Satisfaction/Dissatisfaction and Complaint Behaviour* and *Total Quality Management*.

6

Strategies for improving international students' academic and cultural experience of UK study

Jan Bamford
London Metropolitan University

What do international students think about their educational and cultural experiences in the UK, and what can be done to help them adjust? This research found that there is more for students and institutions to do.

This chapter offers an insight into international students' perceptions of their educational experiences in the UK, and possible solutions for improvements to their learning experiences. Through the use of a qualitative approach and through the themes of language, social and cultural issues that impact on learning processes, the study examines the challenges for international students and the reasons why some find it difficult to adjust to their new environment.

Rationale and Objectives

The challenges presented by the international classroom gave the focus for this research. The research project sought to investigate how international students at London Metropolitan University Business School (LMBS) perceived their learning, what difficulties they were having in making social and cultural adjustments to studying in the UK, if any, and to explore how the university might improve its processes to help these students to cope with their new environment. It was important to try to ascertain and consider possible improvements from the perspective of the students, not just to consider the views and experience of the academics who were their tutors and recruiters. This had particular resonance for the author, who is responsible for the academic experience of the international students on business courses. As Turner (2006) has pointed out, there is a danger of unconsciously imposing our own cultural behaviours and expectations on these students who do not have a working knowledge of UK cultural expectations and behaviours.

Context

London Metropolitan University has a high intake of international and European students, who account for approximately 20% of overall student numbers and, at present, 45% of the student numbers for the Business School. This is not unusual and there has been a corresponding growth in the literature on the international classroom (Carroll and Ryan, 2005) and the 'internationalisation' (Asteris, 2006; De Wit, 2002; Knight, 2006) of higher education which makes the importance of discussion of these issues evident.

There are clearly challenges for international students studying at higher education institutions in the UK. These challenges require higher education institutions to revaluate teaching and learning strategies in the light of the increased recruitment of such students to the UK in order to consider ways in which their experience can be improved.

Description

This case study explores some of the key issues that arose from a research project focused on an analysis of the international student's perception of their experience in a post-1992 university in London. The project used a qualitative approach for the collection of data, through the use of four focus groups, three in-depth semi-structured interviews with postgraduate, undergraduate and semester-only students as well as open-ended questionnaires. The findings were analysed on the basis of the international student experience in the classroom and how international students adapt to the challenges presented by a different educational system, academically, culturally and socially. The term 'international students' is taken here to mean those students who have been educated in a national education system outside the UK and who on the whole are likely to be non-native speakers of English, although this is not necessarily the case.

Evaluative comments

English language ability

A big challenge for international students concerns English language ability, and consideration of those international students who are non-native speakers of English. The minimum language entry requirement for international and European students would normally consist of a specific TOEFL or IELTS score. However, even when students more than meet this entry requirement, they may not be familiar with technical terminology for a specialist subject area.

For some students who have only just achieved the language criteria, studying in English, particularly at masters level, can prove onerous and stressful. Half the students in this case study had only just met the language entry requirement, and for those students the independent study required at a very early stage of the course was problematic. There are those who are so confident of their language abilities that they feel language support classes do not meet their needs: the classes are too generic and what they are seeking is further explanation of specialised terminology.

However, little time is spent in addressing the more specialist support required by these students. As a consequence, these students become frustrated, as lecturers can mistake their lack of specific knowledge in technical (or even political or cultural) terminology for generic difficulties with language. Here is an example of a student expressing this frustration in one of the focus groups:

> They need to know that most postgraduate students were international, there was only one British. They need to understand that we are not English. It is important so they know how to explain things, how to talk to us.

In addition the students have different levels of English, which can hinder the educational experience of the whole group. Another student from one of the focus groups commented that:

> There are some people who come from different backgrounds – I don't know enough about how people are taught in China but we have different levels of English and different backgrounds – some people just receive and don't give.

Not speaking up in class can also make it difficult for tutors to gain a clear picture of the levels of English language ability and the understanding of the students.

Social and cultural adjustment

Volet and Ang comment that 'tertiary institutions have a social responsibility to design learning environments which foster students' developments on intercultural adaptability' (1998: 21). While students did not feel that a lack of social and cultural knowledge of the UK had affected their ability to study, there was a feeling that lecturers should incorporate knowledge of the students' native cultures into their class discussion, as this could benefit everyone.

The focus groups felt that tutors should also not assume background knowledge of political and economic issues in the UK. Others expressed strongly the view that the differences in study methods, compared to their home countries, were a challenge particularly in the first few weeks of their course. Class contribution can also be a traumatic experience but it can be facilitated by tutors who can make the students feel more comfortable in discussing subjects with other students who they don't know. The importance of class interaction for international students is reinforced by Jackson (2003) who comments on the necessity for building a 'considerable rapport' with the group. This rapport is seen as one of the most effective learning and teaching techniques for international students.

Study methods

Differences in study methods compared to the country of origin present a difficulty for international students. In many countries students spend a much greater amount of time in class. There is less emphasis on independent study and more focus on developing the information provided by lecturers in their sessions. Obviously this varies in extent, but many experience a great deal of difficulty with making the required transition in a very short period of time. For example, students have to cope with what is expected of them – usually an increased amount of required reading in another language – as well as developing the ability to synthesise that information in a critical way. They have to achieve this often within the first eight weeks of arriving in the UK and with no further input from tutors until they receive feedback on an assessment.

De Vita (2001) shows the differences of approach used to address a piece of assessment and discusses how the different discourse styles experienced by students from various countries can create tensions that affect a student's performance. Group work may also be an issue – the cultural diversity of groups requires that students acquire intercultural skills which can be an onerous additional requirement in certain business subjects.

It was clear from the focus groups that students from different cultural groups react to these stresses in different ways. There are clearly cultural groups who find class interaction more difficult than others, for example, those from more collectivist cultures. In addition it must not be forgotten that many students are suffering from 'culture shock' and are still trying to adjust to life in the UK when their first assessments are due. As one student put it, 'even little things, like how to submit your essay if you are in a different country are problematic'.

Students commented in some depth about the culture shock that they had experienced and this was exacerbated by the difficulties that many students had in making friends in London. The isolation that many international students suffer as result of coming to the UK to study can vary enormously but it was an ever-present theme. Institutions need to consider the social context of students' adjustment in order to address this isolation.

Discussion

Students' perspectives on the possibilities for improving their experience and suggestions for improvement

Both the focus groups and the interviewees made suggestions about cultural, social and academic aspects of their studies which they felt would improve the student experience.

Byrne, Flood & Willis (2002) comment that the present global environment requires that students be equipped to survive and thrive in a competitive global environment by encouraging them to develop as independent, active and lifelong learners. With this and the findings from the research in mind the following suggestions are proposed to enable international students to make the transition necessary to study in the UK.

Peer mentoring

Hughes and Wisker (1998) comment that the introduction of a mentor (a peer who has already completed the year/term that the new student is starting and who can provide guidance and support) will help international students to cope with their new cultural experience.

The findings of this research indicate a number of areas in which the introduction of a mentor would assist including the communication problems that international students identify. Peer mentoring provides students with a method of communicating with those who have already progressed in their studies. Bamford (2005) analysed the introduction of a pilot peer-mentoring project for international postgraduate students and the feedback was very encouraging. The focus groups indicated that students thought it would be an appropriate addition to student support. Students can offer peer advice on aspects of study such as skills, details on the nature of a subject being taught, help with approaches to assessment as well as provide support for language difficulties and a social framework for studies. The introduction of a peer assisted learning scheme by LMBS has so far proved extremely successfully in offering students an additional support system.

Local language/Study skills group

It was generally felt in the focus groups that communication and interaction between students ought to be encouraged. One of the ways this could be achieved was by encouraging the students to get to know each other in the first semester. Of the comments made by the students interviewed, Student C felt that classes held on study skills and language ought to encourage friendships between the students. Student C felt there would be more context to their study if students knew each other better.

There are clearly challenges for the students surrounding language, for example understanding the accents of other students or even the lecturer's pronunciation. Some students in Focus group D felt that they could simply not understand their tutor's accent as he was not from the UK. As the faculty of an institution becomes more international, another dimension can be added to the problems of communication for all students.

Focus group A said that central language support was inadequate for their needs as it was offered at too basic a level and some of the important information that they needed, such as how to reference properly, was not given. Students identify the importance of study skills and guidance on issues like referencing as crucially important to their learning development. They would value a forum in which they could be encouraged to get to know each other which could facilitate their communication in class.

In response good practice requires that study-skills support is subject specific and if possible course specific, reinforcing the development of students' communication with each other and allowing them to become confident within the context of their specialist study area. When the focus groups and the interviewees were asked what they thought of the introduction of such sessions the responses were very positive.

More social activity

Socialisation was another important theme. Student C commented at great length on the importance of social networks for the Chinese students and the need for the students to feel a sense of identity with the university. The focus groups also felt that there had been a lot of activity in the first week but nothing since then. Some even commented that it had been difficult to make friends although they did not expand on the reasons for this. Comments made by students in the focus groups and interviews clearly reflect the need to develop effective communication between students. The creation of friendships and a social network assist this process by providing students with an identity, both with each other and with the institution.

A study carried out by Hughes and Wisker (1998) found that all the students raised the issue of socialisation. They found that, while the students appreciated the help that they had received in induction, they felt that they would benefit from more assistance, as it would help them settle into life in their institution more easily. In the second part of their study they note that students reported the usefulness of initial and ongoing induction and orientation, both academic, and emotional and cultural. This sort of induction reduces the wastage of 'emotional energy' on 'culture shock'. Again good practice determines the continued resourcing of support for social networks for international students. An easy way to address this, and one that students are willing to engage in, is through the use of internet social networking sites.

Teaching, learning and assessment

The findings of the research clearly touched on aspects of the students' experience that are relevant to teaching, learning and assessment strategies and they highlight how these strategies should take into consideration the additional dimension of the international classroom. The growth in international student numbers in the UK has important implications for the teaching and learning strategies of higher education institutions, particularly those with high levels of international student recruitment. This is the case in the business school, where at least one third of the department's students arrive in the UK from another country.

The focus groups containing Far Eastern students commented on the differences in teaching style between their home countries and the UK. Student C felt that Chinese students' learning styles were initially incompatible with what tutors expected, and that they were too shy to express the difficulties that they were having. Some of the students also felt that they had something to contribute to other students' learning experiences and that tutors need to be aware that the international dimension to the classroom can provide an added benefit. The focus groups felt that this was something that was often ignored.

Swisher & Schoorman (2001) comment on the importance of the tutor having some knowledge of the cultural differences of the students in the classroom. The diverse communication patterns among cultures require that tutors need to be prepared for classrooms where students who dread being called upon by their first name to answer a question sit alongside students from cultural backgrounds which are quite at home with such interactions. They argue that a student's non-verbal communication is important, for example differences in eye contact. In their view, teachers should recognise that their own classroom interactions and expectations are also 'culturally rooted', in the same way as their students. A type of behaviour, or indeed way of talking, may be accepted practice in the UK but to students from a different background it may be detrimental to understanding.

The requirement therefore is to be sensitive to diversity in the classroom without being patronising. The issue of differences in assessment has been mentioned previously and it is clear that teaching and learning strategies need to consider the impact of cultural diversity in the classroom on the teaching and learning process. Institutions need to implement strategies that consider the implications of a high proportion of international students from a variety of cultures where the first language is not English.

Staff development

Biggs (1999) highlights the concept of assimilation as an approach to teaching international students: in other words, international students are expected to assimilate in accordance with our definition of what constitutes a good student. It is here that many of the stereotypes about international students will be reinforced and self-fulfilling. Biggs argues that some of these generalisations are true, but that they could be true of any student (for example 'they don't understand what plagiarism means'); or they are simply untrue (for example, 'they do not easily adjust to local conditions') and that it is generalisations such as these which colour the learning experience.

Another example of misinterpreted-stereotype student behaviour – 'they don't express opinions because their English is poor' – is in fact a generalisation that is often likely to be incorrect, as was demonstrated by the focus-group findings. It was evident from the discussion in Focus group A that students felt pressured to contribute to class discussion but they felt that they should not have to do this if they did not have anything to contribute:

> in one module nobody speaks because we do not know the others and they do not know us ... we are all separates. We are sitting there and the others are sitting there.

The focus groups spoke about the difference in the second semester and how, as students become more comfortable with their surroundings and their peers, they become more confident and relaxed about contributing in class. Turner (2006) also demonstrates the differences between the British archetype student and the Chinese archetype student.

It would be prudent in a culturally diverse institution to provide members of staff with informative sessions on cultural patterns of expression and expectations of learning and to address some of the stereotypical preconceptions of certain cultures in order to increase tutor awareness in the classroom and to improve the student learning experience. Clearly international students feel that lecturers could learn something from the international classroom. This view was expressed in Focus group

A where students felt that tutors were not taking on board the valuable experience of the students in the class which could be used to broaden everyone's knowledge. Gay (2001) provides further evidence of the reluctance of teachers to take on board multicultural issues, however, there was some conflict with that result in this research, as some students clearly felt that staff were aware of their international background whereas others, in Focus groups A and B, did not. The questionnaire results demonstrated that the majority felt that staff teaching styles should take international student backgrounds into consideration. This is an important area for staff development as was demonstrated in the study carried out by Maxwell et al (2000).

Hughes & Wisker (1998) underline the positive effect that staff development can have when dealing with international students. By investigating staff experience in the multicultural learning environment they were able to identify not only difficulties but also strategies for improving the student learning experience. In their study some of the staff were international students themselves and were able to use their experiences to help develop effective teaching strategies. They found that staff development sessions helped people to share experiences, disseminate findings from research and develop suggestions for good practice, such as the most effective socialisation techniques.

Conclusion

This research clearly demonstrates the difficulties that international students have in adjusting to a new academic environment, as well as providing a student perspective on possible approaches for improvement of their experiences.

Universities and departments need to consider the impact of recruiting large numbers of students who are non-native speakers of English, who have been educated in a national education system other than that of the UK or who have non-UK matriculation qualifications or degrees. The institution needs to consider whether teaching and learning strategies should address the specific study needs of these students. Students commented that some had felt that their learning style and the teaching styles used were incompatible, particularly those from the Far East, and that they were too shy to express the difficulties that they were having. In addition, tutors could perhaps evaluate the appropriateness of strategies when assessing cohorts of these overseas students: for example, the use of group work.

It may also be useful for institutions to provide activities for students to encourage the social adjustments they need to make. Students could be encouraged to organise these activities themselves. Social networks are particularly important for students. For example, students from China commented in great depth on the lack of this aspect to their studies. Friendships and social networks are important in helping students feel a sense of identity both with their peers and the university. Developing networks is very difficult in an urban institution, where modular courses highlight the issue of isolation. Many of the home students, for example, do not live 'on campus' and have social networks which exist outside the university environment. They come to class and go home and do not socialise at the university or even know others, and they are in different classes for each of their modules. This is certainly typical of London-based institutions.

Peer-assisted learning is being used more frequently and can prove to be a useful student support mechanism. Students gain a more structured means of communicating with international and UK students who have already progressed on their course. Such mentors can offer advice on aspects of study skills and possible approaches to assessment. This also provides additional social contact with students already on the course.

The findings from the research illustrated that students would like further guidance on aspects such as referencing and study skills in sessions that were subject-specific. When these sessions are held on a voluntary basis, attendance can be an issue and some thought needs to be given as to how to incorporate these into the curriculum. A useful model for first-year undergraduate students has proved to be a compulsory higher-education orientation module. It is common in some countries to incorporate 'communication'-based modules into the curriculum, particularly in business schools, which provide a forum for students to focus on the communication aspects of their studies.

Some consideration could also be given to the different levels of language and possibly different countries of origin of the students. The use of ice-breakers in the first one or two classes is a useful way of getting the students to engage with each other and feel less self-conscious about expressing opinions in front of those that they don't know. Tutors need to be aware that non-verbal communication is also an important aspect of classroom communication, and that there is a need for sensitivity towards cultural diversity in the classroom.

References

Asteris, M. (2006) British Universities: The 'Coal Exporters' of the 21st Century. *Journal of Studies in International Education* **10** (3) Fall pp 224–40

Bamford, J. (2005) Peer Mentoring for international students: theoretical benefits versus challenges of implementation, an educational perspective. Unpublished paper

Biggs, J. (1999) *Teaching for Quality Learning at University*. England: SRHE & Open University Press

Byrne, M., Flood, B., & Willis, P. (2002) Approaches to Learning of European Business Students. *Journal of Further and Higher Education* **26** (1)

Carroll, J. and Ryan, J. (2005) (eds) *Teaching international students improving learning for all.* Abingdon: Routledge

De Vita, G. (2001) The Use of Groupwork in Large and Diverse Business Management Classes: some critical issues. *International Journal of Management Education* **1** (3)

De Wit, H. (2002) *Internationalization of Higher Education in the United States of America and Europe: A historical, comparative and conceptual analysis.* Westport, CN: Greenwood Press

Gay, G. (2001) Effective Multicultural Teaching Practices. In C. F. Diaz (ed) *Multicultural Education for the 21st Century.* London: Addison-Wesley Longman

Hughes, S. & Wisker, G. (1998) Improving the Teaching and Learning Experiences of Overseas Students. In C. Rust (ed) *Improving Student Learning: Improving Students as Learners.* Oxford: Oxford Centre for Staff & Learning Development

Jackson, P. (2003) Ten challenges for introducing Web-supported learning to overseas students in the social sciences. *Active Learning* 4 (1) p 87

Knight, J. (2006) *Internationalization of Higher Education: New Directions, New Challenges.* Paris: International Association of Universities

Maxwell, G., Adam, M., Pooran, J. & Scott, B. (2000) Cultural Diversity in Learning: Developing Effective Learning for South East Asian Hospitality Students. *Cross Cultural Management* 7 (3) pp 3–12

Swisher, K. & Schoorman, D. (2001) Learning Styles: Implications for Teachers. In C. F. Diaz (ed) *Multicultural Education for the 21st Century.* London: Addison-Wesley-Longman

Turner, Y. (2006) Chinese Students in a UK Business School: Hearing the Student Voice in Reflective Teaching and Learning Practice. *Higher Education Quarterly* 60 (1) pp 27–51

Volet, S. E. & Ang, G. (1998) Culturally mixed groups on international campuses: an opportunity for intercultural learning. *Higher Education Research and Development* 17 (1) pp 5–23

Volet, S. E., & Renshaw, P. D. (1995) Cross-cultural differences in university students' goals and perceptions of study settings for achieving their own goals. *Higher Education* 30 pp 407–33

JAN BAMFORD is an academic leader and international student co-ordinator for London Metropolitan University and is responsible for the international strategy of the business school and the support of international students within the school. Her research interests are in the field of the internationalisation of higher education, particularly focusing on the international classroom, the experiences of international students, transnational collaborative links and joint degrees.

7

Managing diversity – an American perspective

Mari Jo Pesch *University of Colorado Hospital, Denver*
and
Patsy Kemp *Oxford Brookes University*

How do US universities work with the challenges of their diverse and
multicultural students? This chapter examines the experience of Marian
University, Wisconsin, an acknowledged pioneer in internationalisation.

The higher education (HE) environment in the United States is becoming increasingly diverse, global, and multicultural (Toossi, 2002). Twenty years ago, the higher education population was predominantly white middle class (Knapp et al, 2008), but there has been a demographic shift, and this, along with an increase in access to technology, has made HE more accessible to an increasing immigrant population (O'Donnell, 2006). When African-American, Hispanic and students from other backgrounds (US Department of Commerce, Census Bureau, 2006) are added to the ethnic mix, lecturers need to keep pace with and be aware of these multiple variations in cultural identity and how this impacts on the student learning experience (Heistad, 2005).

In this chapter, we examine an American perspective on managing diversity in educational groupings, with a look at Marian University, Wisconsin, and more particularly at their Sport and Recreation Management Programme (SRMP) run by the School of Business. Marian has grown over time; it began as a teacher training school in 1851, became a junior university, and was granted full university status in 2008. The current president, Josefina Castillo Baltodano JD, is driving the diversity initiative in Marian. In her inaugural speech she announced that inclusiveness and diversity would be part of Marian's strategic direction. She stated:

> we envision an opportunity to deepen our commitment to Marian's mission by becoming a more diverse institution as reflected in the composition of our board, faculty, staff and students. We envision that Marian will enhance curricular and instructional strategies and university support services responsive to a global world and a diverse student body, with a focus on developing multi-cultural competencies.
>
> (Baltodano, 2007)

Recognising the importance of globalisation and the need to keep pace with the diversification of higher education, in 2008 the university made a decision to adopt a global perspective, supporting core values to promote a culture that fosters intellectual, social and cultural growth in the community and globally.

Marian educators identified the need to develop a global perspective, become literate about diverse cultures and learn how to manage the implications of having more than one culture present in an academic programme. This 'diversity literacy' not only has an influence on the way lecturers approach teaching and programme development; rather, it is a level of awareness, a broader way of seeing themselves and the students who participate in their programmes, that shapes everything they do as educators, from planning and preparation to programme delivery. Through examination of personal cultural assumptions, individuals may realise and discover more suitable approaches to designing and teaching higher education programmes. Subsequently it may be possible to encourage students in turn to consider their cultural assumptions and stereotypes, their cultural programming.

Objectives

We examine the overview and situation in which Marian operates, the model used to explain the university's diversity strategy, what this has meant within the SRMP and finally highlight some of the lessons Marian has learned during the early stages of implementation of this strategy.

Rationale

Marian University is a premier applied liberal arts university located in the Midwestern United States. It offers more than forty undergraduate and graduate programmes and a variety of adult accelerated-degree programmes. Its size permits a very favourable student–faculty ratio of 12.4:1, one of the lowest among Midwestern institutions (Marian University, 2008). Marian's programmes of study are designed to meet a full range of pre-professional and professional academic needs, including business, education, the arts, sciences, nursing and technology. There are 3,000 students enrolled from nineteen US states and twelve countries, representing different ethnic backgrounds. Marian has dedicated itself to creating an accessible, inclusive community honouring diversity in areas such as:

Staff recruitment practices

These focus on retaining, attracting, developing and supporting a more diverse board, management and staff to reflect commitment to becoming a more diverse institution.

Curriculum and pedagogy policy

This policy integrates certain core values: community, learning, service, social justice and spiritual traditions. It guides staff in creating a curriculum infused with multiculturalism, as a way to prepare students for success in a diverse, global 21st century (Marian University, 2008). The goal is to enhance and expand curricular strategies, to focus on developing multicultural competencies and ensure that university support services are responsive to a global world and a diverse student body (Gardenswartz & Rowe, 1998).

Educational access

This refers to the creation of an environment of inclusiveness and diversity through cross-cultural learning and exchange – for the entire campus and the surrounding community.

Office of Equity and Inclusion

An Office of Equity and Inclusion has been established. This office leads the university-wide integrated approach to enhancing intercultural/diversity awareness for students, faculty, staff and the community. This includes leading the social justice committee and developing a plan to address the core value of social justice. The social justice core value is creating individual and societal change which supports the value of dignity, and opportunity for every person. The functions of the social justice committee are:

○ To enrich curriculum and non-curricular activities of the university with cross-cultural experiences.
○ To expand multi-cultural connections in the surrounding community.
○ To promote an appreciation of ecological and social justice among men and women of various racial, cultural and economic groups.
○ To plan inter-group programmes to embody human and cultural diversity among members of the campus as well as the local community.
○ To act as an interdisciplinary resource base to facilitate multi-cultural classroom learning.
○ To assist the university's affirmative action officer in an advisory capacity in order to effectively implement the university's affirmative action and non-discrimination policies.
○ To assist university planning with regard to multi-cultural and ecological issues.
○ To serve as an advisory body to professional divisions of the university regarding social justice/human relations issues.

A major issue faced by SRMP lecturers at Marian is how to keep pace with the diversification of higher education and be effective and successful in addressing the diversity and cultures of students attending their programme.

Context

Over a five-year period (2003–08) SRMP enrolment included 500 students from six different ethnic backgrounds. The university and the SRMP anticipate continued growth in the cultural diversity of students and increased enrolment of diverse students The SRMP is designed to prepare undergraduate students with a background in sports and recreation services management, as well as in the scientific principles of sport. Emphasis is placed on career orientation within the context of a liberal-arts background. Thus the SRMP curriculum combines core business and liberal-arts classes with sport and recreation management classes. The focus is on interacting effectively with various clients in sport and recreation centred enterprises; ensuring fundamental business principles are successfully adapted to the specialised settings of sport and recreation-centred enterprises; interacting effectively with clients to ensure that business philosophies are successfully applied in the field of sport and recreation.

On graduation, SRMP students are qualified to work in a variety of areas such as recreational programming, corporate fitness and management, professional/non-professional sports organisations and sports marketing.

As well as being a diverse group themselves, it is highly likely that these graduates will be working in locations or organisations where handling diversity in their working lives will be a necessary skill. Therefore, the management of diversity in the SRMP at Marian is becoming an increasingly urgent issue.

Figure 1 shows a framework devised to help understanding of five important themes; global perspective is the overarching umbrella theme adopted by the SRMP staff. The four other interrelated themes are means of supporting and facilitating the attainment of a global perspective among staff and students.

Figure 1   Framework for managing diversity

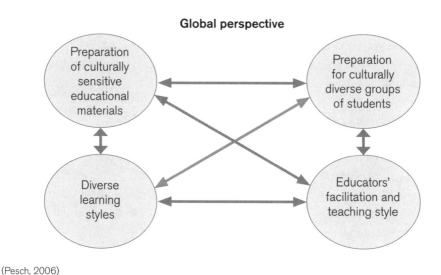

(Pesch, 2006)

Description

Develop a global perspective

SRMP lecturers saw the growing importance of globalisation and an increasingly diverse student population, and they are in the process of developing cultural competence and a global perspective (Bennett & Salonen, 2007). They are intentionally learning about the cultural norms, values, and beliefs of the diverse students they work with. They are developing cross-cultural skills and aspire to become culturally literate which will help them relate to culturally diverse students (Gay, 2000). They are trying to be sensitive and empathetic to student needs. This includes being sensitive to aspects such as customs, values, beliefs and norms – cultural programming, a series of deeply held convictions and emotions which includes, for example, differences in food, language, attitudes towards study, what university life will be: religious practices, beliefs, values, daily habits and others (Pesch, 2006).

This initiative started in 2006 and as we write is still in the process of development. The SRMP lecturers recognise that the questions this approach raises are complex and not easily answered. To achieve this ideal, they are attempting to:

○ Develop some knowledge of the language and culture of the diverse students in the SRMP.
○ Work closely with colleagues from other cultures through, for example, professional and community organisations.

Understanding cultural programming is a complex matter (Anthonissen & Verweel, 2005). The staff at Marian recognise that they need to learn about how different cultures view many aspects of life, for example, self-knowledge. North Americans seek self-knowledge primarily through external sources such as personal therapy, religious affiliations and self-help books whereas people in the United Kingdom and Australia view self-knowledge as a personal act of courage and discovery (Rosen et al, 2000). Knowing that differences of this sort exist and understanding the implications is how the SRMP lecturers aspire to learn to value differences in the world view of their students.

Understand learning styles and culturally diverse students

Research on culturally diverse students and learning styles suggests that lecturers who have developed a global perspective will also be sensitive to the different learning styles culturally diverse students bring to learning events (Dilg, 1999).

Within the Marian context, the SRMP lecturers considered student learning needs and knowledge acquisition processes alongside current resources and facilitation styles. They concluded:

○ It is not enough to be culturally inclusive. Although it is important to take cultural differences into account when planning, developing or facilitating classes, lecturers came to understand that teaching students in the SRMP programme requires knowing about the students' learning styles as well as their cultural values.

○ Getting and keeping students actively involved in learning lies partially in understanding learning-style differences and preferences, so staff see themselves as sensitive to different learning styles and believe that they need to use different teaching or facilitation strategies to work with different learning styles.

Vary educators' facilitation and teaching styles, course delivery format

While the SRMP lecturers know that they need to deal with language differences, dialect and differences in communication patterns, putting all this into place is a challenge. They have a basic belief in the importance of a flexible, facilitative, friendly, sensitive and approachable teaching style. They are keen to implement solutions, but have limited resources. It is expensive and difficult to hire interpreters and find curriculum materials such as books, CDs and videos in multiple languages. Publishers are coming around, but not enough materials are developed yet to meet their needs.

All SRMP lecturers are aware that they need to vary their teaching and facilitation styles whatever the class, but that it is particularly important with a culturally diverse group. They are engaged in setting up the following processes to enhance their ability to teach these groups:

○ Partnering with other lecturers who are successfully teaching culturally diverse students and absorbing their teaching and facilitation methods and strategies. This includes the facilitation of structured warm-up activities, demonstrations, role play and other activity-based learning exercises.

○ Attending professional development programmes to learn about the practices, exercises and techniques lecturers use to increase participation and group learning.

○ Using a variety of computer-based training, experiential activities, games, simulations, case studies, lectures and web-based activities.

○ Learning how to manage highly interactive classrooms and use roundtable discussions, simulations, case study debriefs and action learning sessions.

○ Creating effective hybrid learning models and know-how to develop and integrate curriculum that can be delivered via the Web, face-to-face or through both media.

○ Adapting their curriculum to include role-playing activities which prepare students to work in their home country using formal and informal daily exchanges customary in relevant countries outside the US.

○ Practising cultural etiquette and greetings to use during daily exchanges as part of the course curriculum.

○ Attending educational workshops addressing how to teach and facilitate courses with culturally diverse students.

Preparation for culturally diverse groups of students

Lecturers get to know the students before they start the programme and establish a relationship with them. They make a point of talking to students frequently during course planning and preparation to reinforce student awareness of the purpose, goals, needs and outcomes of the SRMP. They also familiarise themselves with the cultural context of the students and use the US government office of protocol website to learn about the cultures of the students. They read newspapers to see what is going on in the popular culture of the countries represented by the SRMP students.

Design culturally sensitive educational materials

Programme design is consistent with the cultural orientation of the students participating in the sports education programme. Lecturers use and adapt materials that are relevant to participants' actual day-to-day work and life experiences, with names and situations that reflect the cultural mix in the class. Materials also aim to make all students alert to the need for cultural sensitivity in the world of work, and help them to develop an awareness that they may be working in regions where this will be essential.

For example, a case study used in class about a sport marketing manager working in the south-western US will show that they need to know the characteristics of the largely Hispanic population in that region in order to be effective.

Evaluation and current progress

Staff recruitment

Putting this strategy into practice is a challenge, and the faculty are at the beginning of a process which they know will take time. A student-centred approach is key for them, and the department is finding it difficult to recruit lecturers with the work experience and teaching styles which meet the needs of students with culturally diverse learning styles. Current staffing consists of a programme manager, one full-time teaching member and a number of part-time staff. The department are reassessing hiring practice to retain, attract, and develop faculty who can support a more diverse student population as the programme grows.

Student satisfaction

The SRMP faculty and staff are in the initial stages of working with the Office of Equity and Inclusion, focusing on student recruitment and retention. Results from the National Survey of Student Engagement were consulted. (This is a US survey especially designed to provide students and prospective students with information about their undergraduate experience, including views about the quality of education. The survey has a broad scope, with hundreds of colleges and universities of all types and sizes participating each year). Staff are aiming to use the results to learn more about how students evaluate various course elements. They hope that feedback from the survey will guide them in modifying their courses to enhance student learning.

Schedule

The table below shows more detailed information on the current status of the diversity management in the SRMP programme.

Table 1   Initiatives, activities, opportunities to support SRMP diversity strategy

Mentors	Part of first-year student experience; faculty mentor and encourage students to optimise their university experience.
Faculty professional development	Regional and national workshops sponsored by the North American Society for Sport Management (NASSM). The Society promotes, stimulates, and encourages study, research, scholarly writing, and professional development in the area of sport management http://www.nassm.com/.
Guest speakers	A range of guest speakers contribute to the programme, including: ❑ Minor league baseball team manager ❑ YMCA executive directors ❑ NCAA athletic director ❑ Director of guest services, major league football ❑ Alumni from the programme ❑ Directors of a variety of organisations (including resorts with athletic facilities), addressing managing facility, personnel and wellness in profit and non-profit organisations.
Course delivery formats	Discussing blended approach delivery, and investigating platforms that will work with the programme including face-to-face and online. No online delivery, or interpreters currently, but students with learning disabilities are accommodated by providing support tutors, and alternative assessment methods at no cost to the student. This is an area that is also under development.
Course materials	Current materials reflect and emphasise mostly gender equity. Multicultural materials are relatively new. There are five major publishers in sports management and Marian will work with these publishers to ensure textbooks and support materials reflect current population diversity in the SRM field. One or two courses require students to read newspapers or do research online, to research who is being marketed to, 'who they see' and the challenges ethnically diverse employees face in monoculture sport and management organisations. They also consider the trend of diversity in coaching.
Opportunities to study internationally	Nothing is available in sport at the moment, but the university does run a programme elsewhere in the institution.
Service-learning projects (opportunities to participate in the community)	Recreation department runs an after-school youth programme working with kids and provides various opportunities e.g. officiating, proper sportsmanship, management and volunteering. YMCA (family programme) with opportunities for internships, working with the home school students requiring physical education. Internships with minor league baseball teams.

Discussion

In this case study we have identified how staff at Marian have worked towards managing cultural diversity. They are hoping to fully implement the initiative by the autumn of 2009.

This has not been an easy road and it continues to be a challenge. The diversity initiative has come from a university strategic directive and therefore has to be embraced by staff to whom this is a new way of thinking. This presents its own challenges.

Developing a global perspective is not something that happens overnight and requires significant reflection and thought by individuals and groups. Embarking on this path is not always comfortable and requires changes to the ways people deliver their courses. It also requires examination of one's own cultural programming, again a difficult process. A lesson learned is not to ignore the knowledge and experience that students bring to the classroom, but to respect and use it to support learning.

Having said that, through examination of their own cultural assumptions, lecturers may realise and discover more suitable and inclusive approaches to managing cultural diversity which will benefit all students. SRMP staff and lecturers are committed to integrating multicultural materials into curricular and instructional strategies, despite the dearth of multicultural materials (books, simulations, videos, etc.) available from publishers. However, developing their own multicultural instructional materials is time consuming and costly, and with a small faculty, means more programme and course preparation time.

President Baltodano's vision of an inclusive strategic direction to support diversity at Marian requires resources to ensure that staff and faculty efforts and commitment are supported. Marian recognises that they are taking the first steps to promote a culture that fosters intellectual, social and cultural growth in the SRMP, the community and globally, and although the path may be difficult, the effort is already worthwhile and all students, and staff, should see benefit from it now and in the future.

References and URLs

Anthonissen, A. & Verweel, P. (1999) New Questions Concerning Managing Diversity in Sport. *The Cyprus Journal of Sciences* 3 2005

Baltodano, J. C. (2007). Together We Envision. 28 September, retrieved June 16, 2008, from Marian University Web site http://www.marianuniversity.edu/interior.aspx?id=6246

Bennett, J. M. & Salonen, R. (2007) Intercultural communication and the new American campus. *Change* March/April pp 46–50

Dilg, M. (1999) *Race and culture in the classroom: Teaching and learning through multicultural education.* New York: Teachers University Press

Gardenswartz, L. & Rowe, A. (1998) *Managing diversity: A complete desk reference & planning guide.* New York: McGraw-Hill

Gay, G. (2000) *Culturally responsive teaching: Theory, research, practice.* New York: Teachers University Press

Heistad, K. (2005) Developing a culturally competent workforce. *Northeast Human Resource Association*. Retrieved February 20, 2005 from http://www.nehra.comarticlesresources/article.cfm

Knapp, L. G., Kelly-Reid, J. E., Ginder, S. A., and Miller, E. (2008). *Enrollment in Postsecondary Institutions, Fall 2006* (NCES 2008-173). US Department of Education, National Center for Education Statistics. Washington DC: US Government Printing Office.

Marian University (2008) *Mission, Vision and Core Values*. Retrieved June 17, 2008 from http://www.mariancollege.edu/interior.aspx?id=103

Marian University (2008) *University Profile*. Retrieved June 17, 2008 from http://www.mariancollege.edu/interior.aspx?id=325

O'Donnell, K. (2006) *Participation in Adult Education and Lifelong Learning: 2000-01* (NCES 2006077). US Department of Education, National Center for Education Statistics, May. Washington, DC: US. Government Printing Office

Pesch, M. J. (2006) Trainer Perceptions of Culture, Race and Ethnicity on Facilitation of Training Programs: A Global Perspective. (Doctoral dissertation, University of Wisconsin–Milwaukee, 2006)

Rosen, R., Digh, P., Singer, M. & Phillips, C. (2000) *Global literacies: Lessons on business leadership and national cultures*. New York: Simon & Schuster

Toossi, M. (2002) A century of change: The US labor force 1950-2050. *Monthly Labor Review* **125** May pp 15–28. Retrieved March 25, 2003, from http://www.bls.gov/opub/mlr/2002/05/art2full.pdf

US Department of Commerce, Census Bureau (2006) *Current Population Survey (CPS)* October Supplement 1986–2006

Williams, T. & Green, A. (1994) *Dealing with difference*. Hampshire, UK: Gower

MARI JO PESCH is a trainer at the University of Colorado Hospital, Anchutz Medical Campus in Denver, Colorado. In her PhD research, she focused on global perspectives of trainers and trainer perceptions of culture, race and ethnicity on facilitation of training programmes in multinational corporations. Before joining the University, she worked for A C Neilson Marketing Research and taught graduate and undergraduate courses at multiple academic institutions in the United States. As a consultant, Dr Pesch has designed curriculum and facilitated training and educational programmes for school districts, companies and organisations of all sizes, focusing on strategies to build employee skills and knowledge linked to organisation and business needs.

PATSY KEMP is academic developer for the Higher Education Academy Network for Hospitality, Leisure, Sport & Tourism based at Oxford Brookes University. Patsy has intercultural experience in project management, language teaching, business training, and in management consultancy. Before joining the HLST Subject Network, she worked for the Open University, News International (the main UK subsidiary of News Corporation), the World Bank in China and various UK universities. She is the editor, with Nina Becket, of *Enhancing Graduate Employability* (Newbury UK: Threshold Press 2006)

8

Developing intercultural skills for international industries

Judie Gannon
Oxford Brookes University

Hospitality may be an international industry, but do international hotel companies understand intercultural awareness and are the teachers on international hospitality and tourism courses developing these skills?

This chapter reflects on two pieces of research, one undertaken among hospitality and tourism educators and the other across international hotel companies, on the requisite skills and abilities for managing the challenges of internationalisation. It identifies the absence of any rigorous understanding of intercultural awareness and communication skills amongst both sets of respondents despite evidence of the increasing cultural diversity of the customer and workforce profiles in the international hospitality and tourism industries.

Objectives
This chapter sets out to:
○ Review the evidence on the importance of intercultural awareness and intercultural communications skills among contemporary and future hospitality and tourism managers.
○ Present evidence of poor engagement with intercultural awareness and communications skills on international hospitality and tourism management programmes within UK higher education institutions.
○ Highlight the tentative ways in which intercultural awareness and communication skills are used in international hotel companies (IHCs) to recruit, select and deploy future unit general managers (UGMs)
○ Identify the impact these curriculum and people-management lapses will have on the future success of the international hospitality and tourism industry.

The international hospitality and tourism industry
The international hospitality and tourism industry has experienced sustained growth

and generates nearly US $500 billion revenue across the world (WTO, 2007). It is also a major employer and provides jobs and careers for over 350 million people across the globe (ILO, 2001). Although the majority of industry operations are small (in terms of staff numbers) and often independently owned, the industry itself is dominated by several major international companies who have come to dominate the industry via their brand names and service innovations.

The success of these international industry operators is dependent upon developing multiple, broadly replicated services across the world to ensure investor support and market share. Litteljohn (2003) has argued that the hospitality and tourism industry by its very nature is international. However, the extent to which this cosmopolitan dimension has shaped the specific skills required of managers has not been extensively examined.

Intercultural awareness and communication skills

The internationalisation of business is paralleled in our personal and professional lives by more opportunities for individuals to meet, interact and live side-by-side with those from different cultural backgrounds to their own. An understanding that culture refers to our membership of certain groups where values are learned and shared is important for all encounters.

Many researchers now argue that communication between people of different cultures or intercultural communication is imperative for successful performance in the contemporary business world (Chaney & Martin, 2007). Following from this, intercultural awareness is the knowledge and attentiveness that an individual demonstrates about variations in cultural conventions and their ability to act effectively in line with this information.

To develop intercultural awareness and communication skills, several considerations must come into play. Gudykunst & Kim (2003) and Baumgarten (1995) highlight the fact that culture-general and culture-specific approaches to developing these abilities are critical. The culture-general approach focuses upon learning about and training in the generic aspects of culture as well as the knowledge and skills which are transferable across different cultures. Baumgarten suggests that individuals being recruited for positions where intercultural interaction will be important should include culture-general aspects in their immediate training, and that these should be part of the selection criteria. Culture-specific training can then build on culture-general training when the specific location for an assignment or work activity has been identified. These facets of intercultural education and training are reflected throughout the two studies outlined here.

The relative infancy of the subject is perhaps shown in the fact that different terms (transcultural, cross-cultural and multicultural) are often used interchangeably despite the efforts of some researchers to differentiate between them.

International managers' intercultural skills

Operating in international environments demands the ability to cope in diverse and complex situations, and in particular with people who have different values, beliefs and backgrounds (Adler & Gundersson, 2008). The complexity of international work experiences has sadly not helped researchers arrive at a clear and agreed agenda for identifying or developing managers who will work beyond their own national boundaries (Scullion & Collings, 2006). Indeed, while dated, Phatak's comments still seem to capture nicely the extensive nature of international manager requirements, when he suggests an international manager should

> have the stamina of an Olympic swimmer, the mental agility of an Einstein, the conversational skill of a professor of languages, the detachment of a judge, the tact of a diplomat and the perseverance of an Egyptian pyramid builder. And if he is going to measure up to the demands of living and working in a foreign country he should also have a feeling for culture; his moral judgements should not be too rigid; he should be able to merge with the local environment with chameleon-like ease and he should show no signs of prejudice. (Phatak, 1974: 183 in Forster & Johnsen, 1996: 179–80)

The male pronoun is a notable feature as the majority of international managers, generically and in the hospitality and tourism industry, are men (Scullion & Collings, 2006). The importance of intercultural skills among managers has remained prominent in the literature due primarily to the debates on expatriate failure (Forster & Johnsen, 1996). Characterised as the premature return of an international assignee, expatriate failure is seen to have several possible precursors. Harzing (1995; 2001; 2004) questioned the notion of expatriate failure, its definition and the research processes. Instead she argued that the focus be on adjustment (so the chance of failure is reduced), selection procedures (so the most capable people are picked), careful assignment job design (to minimise role conflict and uncertainty), and the provision of effective support systems. Accounts from international managers themselves add further to Harzing's case where expatriates acknowledge the difficulties encountered when working and living overseas in diverse cultures (Le Sueur, 1999; Shay & Tracy, 1997).

Adjustment is seen to be critical and falls into two features of anticipatory (where participants are receptive to previous international experience and cross-cultural training) and in-country adjustment. These replicate the categories of culture-general and culture-specific issues identified earlier where the message is that there should be general realistic expectations about international assignments and the cultural dimensions associated with them to ease managers into any assignment. There can then be a focus on the in-country aspect of adjustment where specialised knowledge on a culture and its language(s) are emphasised.

Intercultural skills amongst hospitality managers

The nature of the hospitality industry also places excessive demands for skills on prospective managers. Johnson (1996: 17) reinforces this when quoting the CEO of an IHC explaining about their 'wish list' for international UGMs to be able to

> combine some craft skills with technical know-how, (especially marketing, finance and languages) with strategic thinking ability, and the following personal attributes; seeks opportunity to learn, acts with integrity, adapts to cultural differences, is committed to making a difference, seeks broad business knowledge, brings out the best in people, is team-oriented (member then leader), problem-solver, innovator, has courage to take risks, is proactive in seeking and giving feedback and accepts criticism and learns from mistakes.

Industry research based on managers' analysis of the required qualities for international hospitality career success highlights that they must demonstrate a range of people and interpersonal skills, including primarily: adaptability, flexibility and tolerance, cultural sensitivity and intercultural competence followed by emotional maturity, industry experience, and self-confidence. International etiquette, an understanding of international business, the ability to work with limited resources and effectively manage stress were judged to be relatively important, while functional and technical skills were rated as the lowest priority for managers. These same studies found that in an international hospitality organisation building managers' cross-cultural skills may be far harder but more important than developing functional and technical skills due to the high level of interpersonal and relational skills required, where host country cultures and the needs of a diverse customer base must be considered.

There is mixed evidence on expatriate failure within the industry. Gilatis & Guerrier (1994) find no evidence of expatriate failure rates on a par with those in the generic literature, but this is contrary to the work of Shay & Tracey (1997) and Kriegl (2000). All these enquiries did rate interpersonal skills, adaptability and flexibility, and motivation to work with different cultures as desirable attributes associated with successful expatriation. Kaye and Taylor (1997) identified a clear association between heightened inter-cultural sensitivity and low levels of culture shock. They also established that cross-cultural training received before and/or after arrival (in China) was related to increased inter-cultural sensitivity.

Intercultural awareness and skills in the management curriculum

The internationalisation of business and management curricula has been widely debated (Stone, 2006; Dahl, 2003; De Vita & Case, 2003) and nowhere more extensively than in hospitality and tourism (Charlesworth, 2007; Hearn et al, 2007). Despite these insights there is no coherent overview of the intercultural management skills provision across hospitality and tourism management education within the UK. Developments in the UK university sector have led to a drive towards increasing numbers of international (non-EU and UK) students. But with growing competition across the world for students, the provision of an enabling environment where international learners can come together is particularly important. Among the concerns voiced about the internationalisation of higher education has been the quality of the learning experience for all students as well as the skills abilities of the universities and faculty themselves to accommodate this more diverse student cohort (De Vita & Case, 2003). As part of her study into the internationalisation of programmes, Black (2004) built upon Hale & Tijmstras' (1990) four aspects which would indicate the true internationalisation of hospitality management education. These aspects are:

○ Faculty
    Faculty exchange
    Undertaking joint international research
    Consultancy and publications with overseas partners
○ Students
    Exchanging students
    Operating double-degree and integrated joint programmes
○ Curriculum content
    Internationalisation of disciplines
    Adding international courses to the curriculum
    Adding language courses
    Providing work or study opportunities
○ International alliances
    Exchanging faculty
    Exchanging students
    Setting up programmes.

However, Black acknowledged that sustaining these dimensions within programmes requires a long-term approach specifically in relation to faculty and institutional investment in internationalisation. In the Devine et al, (2008) study the researchers found that hospitality and tourism academics were eager to include more cultural diversity into their curricula but this needed to be supported by their institution's investment in their development and underpinned by clear policies.

The literature identifies a remit for those involved in developing international hospitality and tourism managers to embrace the internationalisation of the industry by clarifying the intercultural knowledge and skills required to successfully manage a culturally diverse industry. The next sections set out the two studies undertaken by the author to shed further light on the remit for the key corporate and education stakeholders.

Intercultural competence among international hotel general managers

The study of the international hotel general managers began by identifying the scale of the companies' international operations. Senior human resource executives were pinpointed as the main respondents due to their responsibility for the deployment and development of hotel managers. An initial questionnaire to these executives was followed by in-depth interviews and access to company documentation as well as opportunities to observe and talk to administrative teams. Extensive documentation was collected in addition to the eight detailed interview transcripts and other field-work notes. This data was mainly qualitative in nature and analysed using manual and computer-aided techniques. More details on the research methods, findings and analysis can be found in Gannon (2007).

The intercultural aspects highlighted in the research centred round several aspects: localisation, international experience, language skills and cultural awareness, and adaptability and the ability and willingness to move between different countries. One executive summarised this as:

> Someone who will be able to evaluate in different backgrounds, different cultures and who will be able to support and maintain the key values of the international customer and the customer services we provide. By international we mean someone who will be broadminded enough to be able to understand local people, local customers and other cultural things.

The aspect of localisation was endorsed by the respondents who said that while the number of host country nationals (HCNs) in senior unit management positions was increasing, the numbers of international managers would never entirely diminish due to the need to present an international 'face' to their brands.

The level of mobility and international experience of managers was seen as a challenging issue to manage. Aspiring managers had to be mobile and facilitate this mobility through their language ability, eagerness to work and live with other cultures, and their lack of domestic ties. Paradoxically the guidance from the companies often suggested that, to facilitate international mobility, managers had to demonstrate they already had international experience, placing managers in a *Catch-22* – unable to get the international job because they did not have sufficient international experience and only able to get international experience in an international job!

International experience itself was often understood in accommodating ways. For example, growing up in an expatriate family or spending some element of their education in an international school or studying abroad were criteria used to justify international experience. There were frequent observations about the importance of cultural awareness, sensitivity and adaptability, although there was less consistency and clarity about what the companies actually meant by these terms. Instead, it seemed that international experience per se was taken as being representative of managers' cultural awareness and adaptability. This paucity of understanding of cultural awareness and adaptability is repeated even more vividly in the human resource management practices used to manage hotel managers where the companies were reluctant to offer training and development because of the uncertainty of the concepts involved.

Language proficiency amongst international hotel managers was a key characteristic of this occupational group. All companies claimed that the majority of their managers spoke at least two languages. Several companies claimed that their UGMs typically spoke between four or five languages. All the companies agreed that language ability was imperative for international management careers. Language ability in English and at least one other language was described as 'vital' or 'essential' as it offered the opportunity for more flexibility in the take-up of international assignments. Half of the respondents blamed the absence of linguistically competent managers for recent pressures to recruit from outside their companies at general-manager level. The companies with domestic hotel divisions identified that the language ability of their domestic hotel managers acted as the main barrier to their international transfer.

There were some differences identified regarding the numbers of local nationals employed as unit and senior hotel managers. The companies with domestic and budget brands sought more local and younger managers to be appointed at the general-manager level. The companies with the larger, less heavily branded and more international hotels emphasised more forcefully the international dimension to general managers' skills and knowledge.

Overall there was a limited level of understanding about what was meant by intercultural skills. When the companies recruited they were driven by technical skills, acumen and abilities as identified by operations managers. However, intercultural skills were part of the selection criteria for graduate and management trainees but these were identified primarily through family and educational background and language proficiency rather than any more rigorous intercultural competence analysis, such as the IDI (Intercultural Development Inventory).

In terms of supporting international transfers, only one company had developed an in-house preparation pack for managers on international assignments. The other companies all relied upon more ad hoc, short pre-departure visits or peer-support mechanisms. The company, which had developed specialist support material, transferred staff at all levels across the company's portfolio of hotel units. The pack aimed to support relocation and pre-empt culture shock. The HR executive justified this investment following research within the company, and the wider international business and academic community. The pack contained general information on coping in diverse environments and with feelings of alienation and detailed information on the country to which the transferee was relocating, and included a range of information from the price of milk to political, religious and social conventions, with details updated on a yearly basis. The pack was sent to employees as they considered the international transfer to help their decision-making and preparation.

Intercultural competence: the internatonal hospitality & tourism curriculum

In order to establish current practice in intercultural communication skills learning and teaching, an initial web-based survey was used to identify the extent and range of international hospitality and tourism programmes across UK HE provision. Table

1 identifies from the 2006 web survey that international programmes were in the minority of provision at undergraduate and postgraduate levels, particularly in the tourism area.

The programme details for the international courses identified were then scrutinised for their international components, and any intercultural skills they addressed. In particular the researcher examined the course details for graduate attributes, specific modules, support, language provision, work experience, international study exchange, and the use of international cases. All the programmes included clear international components such as: international (work) placements; coverage of the international context of hospitality and/or tourism; and language components. Very few courses explicitly identified the teaching of intercultural skills though the teaching of more general management and interpersonal skills was evident. Although this stage of the project provided some insights it was not possible to distinguish whether intercultural skills were developed as part of their remit solely from the secondary internet sources scrutinised.

Table 1   International hospitality and tourism programmes in UK HE 2006

	Undergraduate		Postgraduate	
	Hospitality (%)	Tourism (%)	Hospitality (%)	Tourism (%)
International	23 (23.3)	17 (12.2)	9 (33.3)	13 (19.7)
Not international	76 (76.7)	122 (87.8)	18 (66.6)	53 (80.3)
Total	99	139	27	66

In order to build upon the documentary evidence a questionnaire was developed and sent to programme directors to establish clearly international and intercultural component coverage. The questionnaire was also made available as an online survey through Survey Monkey©. The response rates were 45% for undergraduate and 25% for postgraduate programmes. The lower postgraduate programme response rate is, however, probably skewed by the number of postgraduate hospitality and tourism programmes which are validated but do not run. These were seen to be reasonable response rates for postal/online surveys.

Across the respondents all showed strong agreement that international programmes prepare students for hospitality/tourism work outside their home countries, in diverse, multicultural environments, and for employment with international hospitality and tourism companies. All respondents identified their programmes included a large proportion of international students (non-EU and UK). Unsurprisingly, all the respondents identified that their programmes were underpinned by international academic research, from the generic international business and management, as well as the specific hospitality and tourism literature.

There was less consistency in the use of international study exchange, international work experience and languages included as programme components. Some programmes included these elements as compulsory, while others mentioned the opportunity to participate in these components. There was less evidence of programmes being delivered by international faculty or using links with international companies to underpin students' learning. Only half the respondents identified that their programme's induction and other course documentation supported cultural diversity. In only two institutions' programmes did intercultural competence form part of the programmes' graduate attributes.

A whole section of the questionnaire explored the internationalisation of the curriculum. It was evident from the responses that exploring the international context of the hospitality and tourism industry through case studies and other teaching materials was fundamental to international hospitality and tourism management programmes across the UK HE institutions surveyed. On all programmes, students were encouraged to look outside their home countries to learn about the international dimensions of the industry. Interpersonal skills were being developed as part of the remit of the programmes but the development of intercultural competence was expected to be achieved through student self-development. All programmes encouraged multicultural group work and this may be considered part of this self-development opportunity.

In terms of developing students' knowledge of cultural differences half the respondents said that the work of Hofstede (2001) and Trompenaars (1993) and other cultural theorists was important as part of their teaching. Over 50% of respondents also said that they assessed intercultural communication skills and that cultural diversity was informally used to enhance students' learning experience. A significant minority (35%) of respondents identified that their universities did not have centralised support for the development of cultural awareness and intercultural skills within their programmes.

Where specific questions were asked about interpersonal and intercultural skills few modules were identified. Most were very generic – such as personal and professional development or supervised work experience – and very much aimed at the interpersonal side but without the intercultural dimension. Several programmes included languages which were seen to be very useful at exploring and challenging students' culturally specific communication skills. When identifying issues relating to the development of interpersonal and intercultural communication skills on their programmes respondents highlighted difficulties in embedding cultural awareness, knowing how to address and teach intercultural skills and also ensure that student groups integrated to maximise the potential learning from these encounters.

The final component of the questionnaire asked respondents to evaluate their most internationally focused module addressing interpersonal and/or intercultural skills. Where intercultural issues were tackled the focus was on raising cultural awareness, exploring communication styles and differences and appropriate behaviour adaptations. Managing conflict was not typically addressed as part of these areas and there was limited, mixed use of critical incidents, role plays, simulations, quizzes and questionnaires and diaries as part of students' learning experiences. These approaches are reinforced by the responses indicating that assessment was focused on knowledge accrual rather than reflection on learning and development undertaken.

Discussion

International hotel managers require an extensive raft of knowledge, skills and abilities; these studies specifically focus on the importance of the international and intercultural dimensions of these competences. The evidence suggests that international adjustment issues are handled by the companies by selecting prospective managers who have 'international' backgrounds. Although the signs of expatriate failure and culture shock in the industry may not be definitive, the suggestion that such recruitment activities inhibit the diversity of the managerial cadre and the overall effectiveness of the companies should be acknowledged.

The curriculum of international hospitality and tourism management programmes has a role to play here in developing more interculturally aware and internationally suitable candidates to challenge this limiting of diversity. There is at the moment very partial evidence of intercultural skills development within hospitality and tourism management programmes in the UK and these studies as well as other enquiries (Devine et al, 2008) argue forcefully for more engagement in this area. As the literature and empirical evidence highlight, intercultural awareness and communication skills are difficult to pin down for academics (Stone, 2006) and international executives. However, it is suggested that the key content to be included in management programmes will develop cultural general knowledge, heightened self-awareness and simulate essential intercultural communication skills. For example the use of IDI or the Cross-Cultural Adaptability Inventory (CCAI) could provide students with valuable personal insights on which to develop their intercultural awareness and communication skills.

Language proficiency appears to be one area where international hotel companies have identified a clear measure for intercultural awareness and communication skills. This aspect may be more challenging for UK management educators as fewer language-proficient students are emerging from the compulsory education system and languages are difficult to fit into an already packed curriculum. However, unless there are allowances made in programme specifications for the development of foreign-language skills most students passing through the UK system will fail to meet a fundamental selection standard for international hotel and tourism companies.

The companies' attempts to localise their managerial staff whilst still retaining some expatriate positions suggest that educators should not only be sustaining the growth in the internationalisation of their student cohorts but extending collaborative provision of their programmes with overseas institutions. In this way, HCNs will receive recognised qualifications which facilitate further career development within the industry. Another facet of becoming an international hotel manager is the importance of mobility, and a willingness to experience a series of different international contexts and customer and staff behaviours. This highlights the point that further use of international study exchange and/or work experience within international hospitality and tourism management programmes would greatly enhance the ability of students to develop their international careers.

Summary and conclusions

There is an extensive body of research which identifies international managers as predominantly male, Western in origin and well-educated. Occurrences of culture shock and expatriate failure as well as managers' personal accounts of working internationally highlight the importance of intercultural knowledge and skills to succeed in these environments. The international hospitality and tourism industry is no stranger to these same issues and debates; in fact evidence suggests that this sector may place even higher value on intercultural competence.

The difficulty of developing a career as an international hotel general manager attests to companies' struggles to pinpoint what they mean by international experience as a selection criterion and their less than rigorous application of measures for prospective managers' levels of intercultural awareness and communication skills. The research presented in this chapter highlights the limits to the development of intercultural awareness and communication skills in international hospitality and tourism programmes currently operating in the UK, although there has recently been more fervent debate about their value. The hospitality and tourism industries are seen as inherently international by nature, yet this chapter shows that company approaches and practices are lacking, and highlights how few undergraduate and postgraduate international hospitality and tourism programmes include intercultural skills development. Finally it recommends some ways in which educators can facilitate a more supportive intercultural curriculum which should enhance the effectiveness of managers entering the industry.

References

Adler, N. J. & Gundersson, L. (2008) *International Dimensions of Organizational Behaviour* 6th ed. Cincinnati: South-Western Publishing

Baumgarten, K. (1995) Training and development of international staff. In Harzing, A. W. & Van Ruysseveldt, J. (eds) *International Human Resource Management*. London: Sage pp 205–28

Black, K. (2004) A Review of Factors which Contribute to the Internationalisation of a Programme of Study. *Journal of Hospitality, Leisure, Sport & Tourism Education* 3 (1)

Chaney, L. H. & Martin, J. S. (2007) *Intercultural Business Communication* 4th ed. Upper Saddle River NJ: Prentice-Hall

Charlesworth, Z. (2007) Educating international hospitality students and managers: the role of culture. *International Journal of Contemporary Hospitality Management* 19 (2) pp 133–45

Dahl, S. (2003) An Overview of Intercultural Research. *SIETAR UK Journal* 10 (1) http://europa-com.com/sietar/members/ldownload.pl?mid=1

De Vita, G. & Case, P. (2003) Rethinking the internationalisation agenda in UK higher education. *Journal of Further and Higher Education* November 27 (4) pp 383–98

Devine, F., Hearns, N., Baum, T. & Murray, A. (2008) Cultural diversity in the curriculum: perceptions and attitudes of Irish hospitality and tourism academics. *Irish Educational Studies* 27 (1) March pp 81–97

Forster, N. & Johnson, M. (1996) Expatriate management policies in UK companies new to the international scene. *International Journal of Human Resource Management* 7 (1) pp 177–205

Gannon, J. M. (2007) Strategic human resources and their management: the case of unit general managers in international hotel companies. Unpublished PhD thesis Oxford UK: Oxford Brookes University

Gilatis, N. & Guerrier, Y. 1994 Managing international career moves in international hotel companies. Chapter 13 in Cooper, C. P. & Lockwood, A. (eds.) *Progress in Tourism, Recreation and Hospitality Management* 5 pp 229–241

Gudykunst, W. & Kim, Y. (2003) *Communicating with Strangers* 4th ed. Boston MA: McGraw-Hill

Hale, A. & Tijmstra, S. (1990) *European Management Education*. Geneva: INTERMAN

Harzing, A. W. K. (1995) The Persistent Myth of High Expatriate Failure Rates. *International Journal of Human Resource Management* 6 May pp 457–75

Harzing, A. W. K. (2001) Of Bears, Bumble-Bees and Spiders: The Role of Expatriates in Controlling Foreign Subsidiaries. *Journal of World Business* 36 (4) pp 366–79

Harzing, A. W. K. (2004) Composing an International Staff. Chapter 10 in Harzing, A. W. K. & Van Ruysseveldt, J. (eds) *International Human Resource Management* 2nd ed. London: Sage pp 252–82

Hofstede, G. (2001) *Culture's consequences: Comparing values, behaviors, institutions, and organizations across nations*. Second edition. Sage: Beverly Hills

Trompenaars, F. (1993) *Riding the waves of culture: Understanding diversity in global business*. New York: Irwin

International Labour Office (ILO) (2001) *Human resources development, employment and globalization in the hotel, catering and tourism sector*. Report for the discussion at the Tri-partite Meeting on the Human Resources development Employment and Globalization in the Hotel, Catering and Tourism Sector Geneva: ILO

Kaye, M. & Taylor, W. G. K. (1997) Expatriate Culture shock in China: a study in the Beijing hotel industry. *Journal of Managerial Psychology* 12 (8)

Kriegl, U. (2000) International hospitality management. *Cornell Hotel and Restaurant Administration Quarterly* 41 (2) April pp 64–71

Le Seuer, A. (1999) *Running a hotel on the roof of the World: Five years in Tibet*. Chichester: Summersdale Publishers

Litteljohn, D. (2003) Hotels. Chapter 1 in Brotherton, B. (ed) *The International Hospitality Industry: Structure, Characteristics and Issues*. Oxford: Butterworth-Heinemann pp 5–29

Maxwell, G., Adam, M., Pooran, J. & Scott, B. (2000) Cultural Diversity in Learning: Developing Effective Learning for South East Asian Hospitality Management Students. *Cross Cultural Management* 7 (3) pp 3–12

Scullion, H. & Collings, D. G. (2006) eds *Global Staffing*. London: Routledge

Shay, J. & Tracey, J. B. (1997) Expatriate Managers: Reasons for failure and implications for training. *Cornell Hotel and Restaurant Administration Quarterly* February 38 (1) pp 30–5

Stone, N. (2006) Conceptualising Intercultural Effectiveness for University Teaching. *Journal of*

Studies in International Education 10 (4) Winter pp 334–56

Trompenaars, F. (1993) *Riding the waves of culture: Understanding diversity in global business.* New York: Irwin

WTO (2007) World Tourism Organization *Trends in tourist markets.* Madrid: World Tourism Organization

JUDIE GANNON is senior lecturer in the Department of Hospitality, Leisure and Tourism Management at Oxford Brookes University. Her teaching and research interests focus upon international human resource management, internationalisation and intercultural awareness and communication skills, at both undergraduate and postgraduate levels. Dr Gannon is currently studying for a postgraduate qualification in mentoring and coaching and is eager to undertake further research on the impact of coaching and mentoring across cultures.

9

Designing a full-time masters programme for a culturally diverse student population

Melanie Weaver, Angela Vickerstaff and Malcolm Sullivan
Nottingham Business School, Nottingham Trent University

To promote international student learning Nottingham Business School moved away from the traditional design of a masters-level programme towards a more innovative, themed curriculum structure, to meet the needs of their culturally diverse students better.

Objectives

The following objectives were behind the development of the course:

○ To offer a specialist post-graduate course in marketing that is both practically and academically relevant and prepares students for a career in marketing.

○ To help students to enhance and develop their knowledge through providing a critical but supportive learning environment that meets the needs of a diverse multi-cultural cohort.

Rationale

Two quite popular misconceptions in the UK HE sector are that international students can be seen as homogeneous and that the standard UK model of HE delivery fits all of them. Research carried out into the various customer groups (De Vita, 2000; Kember, 2000; Spencer, 2003) shows that international students are far from homogeneous – in fact, highly heterogeneous – and that the traditional UK HE model may be cost-effective to deliver but doesn't satisfy all the specific needs of international students. Thus the course team were keen to develop a masters course that would more effectively meet the needs of our international student body.

A number of key inputs contributed to the analysis phase of the programme's development, namely: relevant academic research into the education of a diverse multi-cultural cohort, marketing education (Clarke & Flaherty, 2002) and current issues challenging or augmenting the marketing theory base. In addition, marketing research was undertaken to build an understanding of the key target customers, the competition, the dynamics of the market and internal considerations.

Informed by this research, a series of 'guiding principles' were proposed, many of which focused on the international nature of the student cohort (see Table 1).

Table 1   Guiding principles for the MSc Marketing degree

Guiding Principles	Basis
International full-time students share many similarities with part-time students in the UK, and hence should be treated in a similar way	Their 'job' is to learn the language, culture and academic system and this is no less challenging than any work life balancing exercise.
Masters-level study requires students to learn and reflect independently hence a strong guided-study culture is essential (e.g. scheduled pre-entry and study prior to, during and after modules)	Some students may be unfamiliar with constructive learning, and may take time to adjust to the new learning environment. Directed study helps students to use their time effectively. It takes them through the learning and critical thinking processes, encouraging them to prepare for sessions and hence building their confidence to contribute to class discussions.
Small group learning allows for input to be tailored to meet more effectively the needs of a diverse multi-cultural cohort	Small group teaching emphasises peer learning, which is often highly motivational for international students. It offers lecturers flexibility to better meet student needs. It provides a less intimidating learning environment for international students to engage critically with materials, and can help students to develop their social and communication skills.
The ideal teaching and learning environment should be mutually beneficial and supportive, yet stimulating	All learning environments should be stimulating for students. International students will also need time and support to adjust to a new learning environment. Tutorials and group work provide a supportive environment.
Achievement at masters level is not simply measured by the quantity of assessment	Quality of assessment is a vital consideration, especially for international students where over assessment can often be counter-productive. Instead, balance of assessments in terms of type and volume is necessary to more effectively assess student learning.

Context

Nottingham Trent University (NTU) is a leading, large and well-established post-1992 university with considerable experience of educating international students both in the UK and across the world. This experience comprises the recruitment of international students on to a range of undergraduate (UG) and postgraduate (PG) programmes delivered at NTU, as well as a range of collaborations overseas resulting in a range of NTU supported programmes. In common with the majority of UK HEIs, non-EU students are an important income stream for NTU and thus its provision is structured accordingly. Nottingham Business School (NBS) accounts for a significant proportion of the University's international student recruitment and each year welcomes such students on to a number of UG and PG courses. Historically these courses have been structured to suit a predominantly UK student body. Recent strategic initiatives have sought to redress this imbalance by making programmes more international in nature.

Looking at the market, demand for PG marketing degrees amongst non-EU students continues to be strong despite recent reductions from key markets such as China. Whilst these key markets (e.g. China, India, Thailand and Taiwan) still have great importance for UK HEIs, the typical UK PG marketing programme attracts students from a broad range of countries, cultures and educational backgrounds. On the supply side, currently between 75 and 100 competing programmes are offered by UK institutions. These programmes are remarkably similar in structure and teaching approach, with one-year programmes based on the traditional UK-taught PG-programme model (large-group lectures, some seminars and workshops, high levels of assessment and a significant amount of assessment by examination) accounting for the vast majority of the total.

This degree of programme homogeneity would seem to suggest that the needs of non-EU students are homogeneous and similar to their UK counterparts. Published academic research combined with research conducted within NBS and a considerable number of years of accumulated experience in teaching non-EU students challenge this assumption and led NBS to identify some key points of difference (see Table 2).

Table 2   Basic needs of international students

Time and support to adjust to an unfamiliar social environment
Time and support to adjust to a different academic environment
Guidance on the requirements of assessment at masters level in the UK
Additional time to assimilate information
Additional time to prepare assessments
Recognition of their unique cultural experiences as a valid input into the teaching process
Recognition of how prior learning experiences may only partially prepare them for HE learning in the UK

When reading this table, it should be noted that students' countries of origin will introduce additional culturally-specific requirements that need to be satisfied if the programme is to be successful. For example, some cultures place a higher value on relationships with teaching staff than others. The design challenge therefore, is to produce a programme that can meet the basic needs that apply to all international students and be sufficiently flexible and adaptable to meet the higher level needs of specific international student groups.

Designing and delivering the programme

The programme was designed to adhere to the guiding principles and meet the needs of the diverse, multi-cultural cohort. The key design features are explained below.

Mode of attendance, duration and start date

Based on market and customer analysis, it was decided that the programme would be of one year's duration, commencing in September. It would operate on a full-time basis as this matched customer requirements as the preferred model in the majority of international markets. But also, and perhaps more critically, this complied with study-visa requirements on the number of study hours per week. Further support for this model was found by analysing existing provision in the UK. With a couple of exceptions, programmes have a main start date in line with the academic calendar and run for 10 to 12 months.

The curriculum structure

The programme would commence with a two-week induction period. Delivery would be based on three-hour sessions, about 15 hours per week, with the aim of 'easing' students into the UK and university culture, providing them with programme details, meeting the teaching team, introducing them to facilities and services, and holding discussions and activities around cultural issues and study skills.

The programme itself would be structured around the sequential delivery of six thematic modules, plus one 'long and thin' research module (*Marketing Studies*) delivered throughout the year, as in Figure 1 (below).

Figure 1   MSc Marketing curriculum structure

Marketing Studies (60 cps)	Contemporary Issues and Marketing 20 credit points (cps)
	Marketing Contexts (20 cps)
	Operational Marketing (20 cps)
	Marketing in the Organisation (20 cps)
	The Customer Experience (20 cps)
	Strategic Perspectives (20 cps)
	Induction Programme

This structure would tend to contradict the traditional paradigm of a functional approach and would thus make the programme significantly different from the UK norm outlined in the context section. The functional approach emphasises teaching traditional marketing subjects, which are then supported by various functional or contextual options. The proposed approach, in contrast, would explore core marketing tasks (and *Operational Marketing*), and emphasise the diverse range of external and internal environments (*Marketing Contexts* and *Marketing in the Organisation*). Much of the 'new' material in the *Contemporary Issues and Marketing* module would be practitioner-led, where research is trying to keep abreast of practice. As a final point, the *Marketing Studies* module would provide the research component required at this level of study. To arrive at this outcome, the academic members of the marketing group absorbed the relevant academic and market research, considered the wider debates taking place within the marketing academic community and came to the conclusion that a more innovative, themed approach to curriculum delivery was required.

This view is supported by prior research which highlights the limitations of whole or large-group instruction: by its very nature, it emphasises uniformity rather than diversity and discourages independent learning. Similarly, in preference to a teaching and learning strategy dominated by large group-lectures, De Vita & Case (2003: 393) suggest that 'helping students construct understandings that are progressively more mature and critical' through small group instruction is more appropriate for teachers who are addressing the needs of a heterogeneous group.

Consideration of the teaching and learning capabilities and preferences of the target students was essential if the programme was to meet the needs of international students. It was anticipated that students might require support and guidance, particularly in the early stages of the course, if they were to be comfortable operating in a student-centred learning environment. With that in mind, and supported by prior research (Abrami et al, 2000), small group teaching would be a central feature of the teaching and learning strategy.

The traditional lecturing method of one-way communication directed at large groups of students was considered not to be appropriate. Therefore, contact within modules would take the form of whole class delivery, small group tutorials and structured guided study. The intention was that each of the six thematic modules would have a mix of these three elements (typically 10 three-hour lectures interspersed with four three-hour small group tutorials over six weeks per module) while the *Marketing Studies* module would be delivered via three-hour tutorials and guided study only. A typical six-weekly delivery pattern would therefore be structured as in figure 2 below.

Figure 2   Typical delivery block

Week 1	Week 2–5	Week 6
Pre-work	Module sessions	Post-work
M A R K E T I N G	S T U D I E S	T U T O R I A L S

The use of pre-work was related closely to the feature of small group learning. Pre-work was advocated to allow students the opportunity to read and assimilate materials prior to the class, which is believed to encourage motivation (Kember, 2000). Their understandings and ideas can then be shared and challenged within a small group teaching environment, again encouraging active learning.

A range of interventions was planned to provide developmental opportunities for students, since it cannot be assumed that students from different countries will respond universally to differing teaching methods (De Vita & Case, 2003; Clarke & Flaherty, 2002). These would include: directed-learning activities, lectures, small group discussions, presentation of seminar papers, academic readings, guest lectures, videos, case studies, practical exercises, field research and e-supported guided study.

The needs of home students were also considered. Previous experience suggested that, whilst home students may feel more comfortable with the teaching and learning environment, they still need support to understand the nature of learning at masters level. In addition, home students can become frustrated at working with international students, failing to appreciate the contribution to learning which a culturally-diverse student cohort can provide. Therefore, the strategy for home students would focus on three needs: developing an understanding of the requirements of the constructive learning environment; providing tailored feedback and learning exercises to challenge individuals' thinking; and reinforcing the benefits of sharing multicultural experiences to develop a deeper understanding of cultural issues.

Assessment

In the same way that students show diversity in their preferred teaching methods, so too assessment methods are considered to be culturally sensitive. Previous experience and research (De Vita, 2002) suggested that assessment by way of examination penalises international students by placing them at a particular disadvantage in comparison to other forms of assessment. Thus, a combination of assessment methods excluding examination was chosen to build student confidence and capabilities.

The intention was to incorporate both formative and summative assessment within modules and progress from shorter, small group-based assessment to larger, individual assessments through the duration of the programme. Group work was considered to be an important feature of the teaching, learning and assessment strategy, whilst recognising that it does not always operate smoothly. Within NBS a range of practices have evolved in order to improve the effectiveness of group work and ensure that group assessment is fair. Table 3 outlines the assessment schedule.

Evaluation of the MSc Marketing programme

The programme was launched in September 2006 with 25 registered students. Of these, 21 students successfully completed in September 2007, with one further student achieving completion in April 2008. With two students having failed, and one student deferring, the programme has achieved an 88% completion rate which compares favourably with other postgraduate programmes in the UK.

Qualitative research was conducted in July and August 2007, after students had completed the taught element of their course, with the aims of determining the success of the inaugural implementation of the course and evaluating students' perceptions, beliefs and attitudes towards the design of the programme and their learning

Table 3   Assessment schedule

Module title	Credit points	Element and weighting
Strategic Perspectives on Marketing	20	Group* Coursework Report (100%)
The Customer Experience	20	Group § Coursework Report & Presentation (100%)
Marketing in the Organisation	20	Individual Coursework Essay (100%)
Operational Marketing	20	Individual Coursework Report (100%)
Marketing Contexts	20	Group § Coursework Presentation (100%)
Contemporary Issues & Marketing	20	Individual coursework essay (100%)
Marketing Studies	60	Individual Coursework Essay (15%) Group Report (25%) Individual Research Paper (60%)

Notes: * Group Size = 4–5, § Group Size = 2–3

experiences. Three focus groups were initially run, with a total of 20 participants, and subsequent interviews were conducted with two female and two male students. The research findings are outlined below.

Induction

The two-week induction was the first opportunity for staff and students to meet, with students particularly enjoying the social and cultural aspects of their induction, such as role plays, team building and ice-breaking activities. They felt more prepared and confident about working in group activities. However, they wanted less 'information' but more marketing content within the induction, more contact time each day and a shorter induction period.

The course team had assumed that students were 'fresh off the boat' and needed time to adjust to their environment. This proved not to be the case as students had generally been in the UK for a number of weeks, months or even years, either as visitors, or as students on short language courses or first degrees. Many of them also had family or support groups picking them up on arrival, and helping them to get acclimatised to the UK. Suggested improvements for induction were an increased focus on study and masters-level skills, more team building and social activities, and an introduction to British culture.

Relationships

All students felt that developing relationships with both staff and fellow students was a valuable part of the experience. They felt that the friendships made with their peers were strong, and they particularly valued learning about different cultures. They commented on the 'good' relationships they had developed with most of the lecturers from contact in tutorials. Asian students said they appreciated the friendliness of the staff and being on a first name basis with them, although the more informal and relaxed climate caused problems as well.

For much of the year some students felt uncertain about university culture and norms which were not made explicit. They did not realise, for example, that they could meet with lecturers outside class time. In addition, the efforts of the course leader to accommodate early requests (e.g. for moving tutorial groups) led to increasing complaints and demands for change. This more 'casual' environment also resulted in increasing tardiness, and reduced concern for following rules and guidelines (e.g. many students stopped doing required pre-reading when they realised they wouldn't be 'tested' specifically).

Students were also quick to note any occasional lack of communication between lecturers about lecture content across modules, unpreparedness on some tutorial activities or their limited variety. In some instances, this reduced their respect for the programme and individual lecturers.

Delivery modes

Lectures were accepted as a familiar mode of delivery. Some students were 'more comfortable' with this style of teaching, although there were mixed views about the three-hour blocks of teaching. They generally agreed that their ability to listen and absorb new information for three hours depended primarily on the subject but sometimes on the lecturer's style of delivery, or on an individual student's ability to process the English language or even the accent of the lecturer. In conclusion there was no agreement as to the 'best' length of time for whole-group teaching.

Small group teaching was universally seen as valuable. Students appreciated clarifying understanding, expressing views directly with tutors and peers and conducting structured activities in a supportive environment. Those with more difficulty expressing themselves verbally particularly appreciated small-group and directed teaching as they felt less pressured.

Group assessment was a popular theme and was regularly discussed. Students felt they had not received enough instruction on different cultures and particularly team roles, however others believed that no matter what one learned in theory, it was always going to be difficult to put into practice: learning came from experience. It was also suggested that problems in groups arose from clashes in personalities rather than cultural differences. With the benefit of hindsight, some students saw group assessment as a valuable learning experience.

Studying and living in the UK

Some students stated that they expected the learning style to be different in the UK and were willing to embrace it. In addition, the sequential nature of the course was appreciated by the majority of students, although some (those with weaker language skills) found the pace difficult to cope with at first. However, all agreed that it became easier as the course commenced. Over time, as they became more familiar with course expectations and received relevant support from staff and their peers, most students showed significant progress towards a more constructive learning style.

Students said that they did not tend to socialise away from the course; they did not engage with UK culture beyond staff and fellow students. Assumptions were made by academics and students that they would learn about and integrate into British culture through social interaction with their fellow home students. The reality was that learning about British, or at least Western, culture came primarily through lecturers. Whilst friendships grew between individuals, much of the international students' free time was spent on their own, communicating with friends and family via the internet. This resulted in a number of students feeling lonely and isolated. In fact, a number of students travelled home during the longer breaks from classes, which of course reduced the chances of assimilating into UK culture. A further consequence was the impact on the level of motivation with one student suggesting that he became demotivated when feeling homesick.

Student motivation was variable. A number of students acknowledged they could be 'lazy' and didn't do the pre-work or module-reading recommended, particularly as there were no direct measures of their activity in these areas. This may have been partly as a result of a weak connection between pre-work and tutorial activities at times; more effective links between the reading and required activities may stimulate motivation. On the other hand, students agreed that they were motivated primarily by assessment and one suggested that more 'tests' in class would motivate: 'they won't like it but they'll do it!'

Overall perceptions of the course

Students were decidedly positive about their experience on the programme. Most felt that they had had a great learning experience, with one student going so far as to say it had changed his life! Students reported developing their presentation, research and team-working skills, along with improved spoken, and to a lesser extent, written English. They said they had broadened their understanding of different cultures within their peer group. In particular, all agreed they had become more confident individuals as a result of the programme.

The balance of Asian students to other cultures on the course was an initial concern to some students. Interestingly, this feeling was expressed primarily by the Chinese students who comprised a large segment of the student population (32% Chinese and 28% Taiwanese). Some students had purposely searched for a UK university which had a low ratio of Chinese students to British students to develop British friendships and improve their English communication skills. Although statistically we do have a low ratio of Asian students, that applies to the whole campus and not full-time business masters programmes. However, this attitude had softened by the year-end as friendships developed and students reflected that it was the relationships that were important, not the predominance of one cultural group.

Discussion

From the programme team's point of view, the overall aims and objectives of the programme design have been met although some adjustments inevitably needed to be made. Some changes to delivery or other programme details were made as and when student (and staff) feedback was received throughout the year. Other changes have now been incorporated into this year's delivery, and so far seem to have improved the students' (and academics') learning and teaching experiences, but this will be determined more clearly by results, and evaluation at the culmination of this year's programme, when another review is planned.

Based on this initial success, the programme team have a number of opportunities and also challenges for the future. The second year's intake has already seen a 32% increase in international students; if, as predicted, this growth continues, one challenge for the programme will be to preserve the current culture of a small, friendly and supportive programme with well developed interpersonal relationships.

One way to address this, which has been discussed as a good opportunity, would be to use this new structure as a common platform for developing different postgraduate marketing routes. Synergies would be provided by offering the first three modules as core, and contextualising the *Marketing Studies* module. Given the current climate, the challenge will be to continue to receive approval for programmes based on a design which advocates non-traditional delivery, and needs a higher staff to student ratio than traditional structures.

References

Abrami, P. C., Lou, Y., Chambers, B., Poulsen, C. & Spence, J. C. (2000) Why Should We Group Students Within-Class for Learning? *Educational Research & Evaluation* 6 (2) pp 158–79

Clarke, I. and Flaherty, T (2002) Teaching Internationally: Matching Part-Time MBA Instructional Tools to Host Country Student Preferences. *Journal of Marketing Education* 24 (3) pp 233–42

De Vita, G. (2000) Inclusive Approaches to Effective Communication and Active Participation in the Multicultural Classroom. *Active Learning in Higher Education* 1 (2) pp 168–80

De Vita, G. (2002) Cultural equivalence in the assessment of home and international business management students: a UK exploratory study. *Studies in Higher Education* 27 (2) May pp 221–31

De Vita, G. and Case, P. (2003) Rethinking the internationalisation agenda in UK higher education. *Journal of Further and Higher Education* 27 (4) November pp 383–98

Kember, D. (2000) Misconceptions About the Learning Approaches, Motivation & Study Practices of Asian Students. *Higher Education* 40 pp 99–121.

Spencer, A. (2003) Facilitating the Academic Success of International Students. *Teaching Theology & Religion* 6 (3) pp 164–68

MALCOLM SULLIVAN is the head of the Marketing, Retail and Operations Division of Notthingham Business School, which he joined in 2002. He entered higher education in 1993 after a number of years in consultancy, combining lecturing and research with his consultancy interests. He is still actively engaged in contract work, which directly informs his teaching and research activities. As a principal lecturer, his main teaching interests are in the fields of marketing strategy, retail marketing and buyer behaviour, at postgraduate and corporate level. Malcolm's main research interests are in retail marketing and strategic marketing.

ANGELA VICKERSTAFF joined NBS in 1994, and is a principal lecturer teaching both marketing and research across a wide range of undergraduate, postgraduate and corporate programmes. Dr Vickerstaff has held a number of course management roles within Nottingham Business School, and was responsible for developing a number of postgraduate courses including the MSc marketing. She is currently the division coordinator for commercial work within the Marketing, Retail and Operations Division. She teaches across the NBS portfolio, but her specialist areas are research in marketing and marketing implementation. Angela's doctoral research was in the development of marketing in transforming economy firms. Other interests lie in the area of teaching and learning, particularly the teaching of international students and the development of academic skills.

MELANIE WEAVER joined Nottingham Business School in 1995 from a career in the private sector, spanning industries in the UK and Canada. As a senior lecturer, Melanie teaches strategy and marketing subjects across a range of undergraduate and postgraduate courses. She is programme leader of the Flexible MBA, and module leader of several marketing modules including operational marketing (MSc Marketing). She has a postgraduate certificate in higher education, which initiated her interest in learning and teaching research, with particular focus on student perceptions and the international student experience.

10

Assessed mixed-nationality group work at a UK university: does it get results?

Rachel Wicaksono
York St John University

Are students' views of group work borne out by the results
that students achieve? This chapter contrasts well known
stereotypes with the objective scores, with unexpected results.

This two-phase mixed-methods study explores the benefits and drawbacks of mixed-nationality group work for students at York St John University (YSJU).

The first phase surveys business management students on their experience of group work. I find that certain differences within groups are considered to be negative, including:

○ culture (nationality)
○ (lower) 'proficiency' in English
○ (lower) ability
○ (lower) motivation.

None of these four differences are categorical variables, rather they are scales of belief, behaviour and achievement. I therefore conclude that intra-group difference *per se* may not explain a group-work effect. Instead, I suggest that group outcomes are a result of members' understanding and use of intra-group difference; their context, task and time-dependent *perception* of diversity. I predict that research into intra-group diversity will continue to produce inconsistent results.

The second phase focuses on a threat to equity mentioned in phase one: different levels of intra-group academic achievement. I analyse individual and mixed-nationality group marks from the same cohort of students. Regression of individual marks against group marks finds that the highest-achieving student contributes most to the performance of the group. Further tests show that low and average-achieving students are dragged up by mixed-nationality group work, while the highest-achieving student in the group is dragged down. I suggest that there is some evidence for an information-processing or 'pooling' benefit for most of the group, but not a sufficiently strong 'synergy' or 'teaching effect' to affect the marks of the best students.

I conclude with some suggestions for changes to the organisation and assessment of group work. Under the headline 'Teamwork gets results' the Career section of *The Times* reports:

> As companies adopt a more global outlook, greater collaboration is a vital corporate need.   (Ford, 2007)

> a diverse workforce makes both moral and, increasingly, economic sense.   (Dight, 2007)

In my experience, students at YSJU seemed to dislike working in diverse groups. Discussions with colleagues at other universities suggested that this was a widespread feeling.

Aims of the study

The theme of this study is the construction and use of ideas about 'difference' in learning groups. In the study, I examine students' beliefs about how differences within their groups may account for the benefits and difficulties they have experienced. From the range of ideas expressed by students about difference in learning groups, I select the category 'ability' and describe the relationship between individual and group marks, on a module of study at YSJU.

The first phase of the study aims to answer the research question:

○ What do students (home and international) enrolled in a BA Business Management at YSJU think about group work?

The second phase of the study aims to answer the research question:

○ Does having higher ability students in the group increase the group mark or does group work drag everyone's marks down?

That is, to what extent is achievement in group work (where grades are based on group performance criteria) a function of the individual achievement (as shown in other individual, i.e. non-group, assessments) of group members?

Group member diversity and group performance

At least five decades of research into the relationships between group membership and group performance have found positive, negative and neutral effects. Explanations of group performance have been offered in psychology, education and economics, and include the theories of: similarity-attraction, social identity/self-categorisation, information-processing (Mannix & Neale, 2005), peer effect (Hoxby, 2000; Ding & Lehrer, 2005) and 'free riding' (Pitt, 2000). Beliefs about the teams' resources, external forces (institutional, local, national), as well as time, task type and expectations of group work, may also mediate interaction between group members.

One aspect of group input that has received a great deal of attention in the literature is the level of diversity within the group. Mannix and Neale (2005) cite research that both supports and contradicts the claim that teams with surface-level diversity – race, ethnicity, gender, age, language(s) – may not function as effectively as superficially

Table 1   Conceptual framework for mixed-group work research

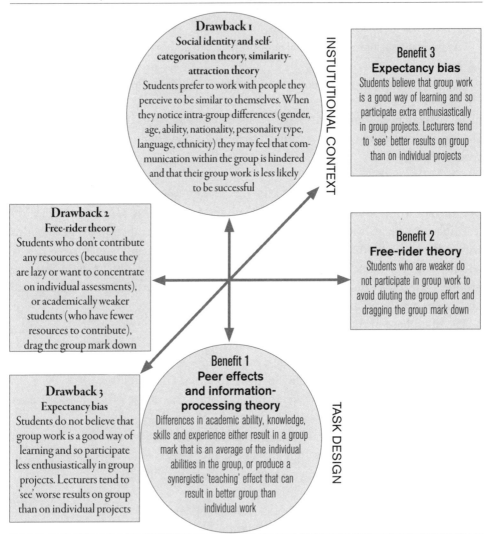

homogenous teams. They suggest that this lack of consistency between findings could be because groups' *perception* of intra-group diversity affects if, and how, the group decides to interact. Mannix and Neale define diversity as, 'any attribute people use to tell themselves that another person is different.'

The diagram aims to summarise these explanations and show how they relate to each other. Explanations for the possible drawbacks of group work are shown in serif font, while explanations for the possible benefits are shown in sans serif font. The lines on the diagram show how theories of positive and negative group-work effects can be ranged on a number of axes, as well as how they may be dependent for their effect on the institutional context and task type. The interaction of the axes is an attempt to show that, while the theories presented in the literature review have been, on the whole, presented in isolation from each other, it is possible that they could co-exist, reinforcing or cancelling each other out.

Research design and theory

The conceptual framework above, developed from the literature on mixed groups, is used to analyse data collected from YSJU business management students on their experiences of and beliefs about group work. The analysis of the qualitative data finds that students experience difference in terms of language, nationality and ability and fear that these differences have a negative effect on their group mark. The literature on peer effects of group work shows that students' fears about their marks being dragged down by weaker students are probably unfounded, and so in the second stage of the study I deduce and test three hypotheses about the relationship between the ability of individual members and the group mark.

Tashakkori and Teddlie (1998: 46), call this design a two-phase, QUAL/QUAN, 'sequential mixed methods' design. They say:

> In the QUAL/QUAN sequence ... the investigator starts with qualitative data collection and analysis on a relatively unexplored topic, using the results to design a subsequent quantitative phase of the study. (1998: 47)

The theoretical underpinnings of a mixed methods approach are pragmatic (Tashakkori & Teddlie, 1998; Robson, 2002). Rejecting the either/or choice of positivism (including post-positivism) and constructivism, the pragmatic paradigm 'embraces both points of view' (Tashakkori & Teddlie, 1998: 23). Employing both inductive and deductive logic, qualitative and quantitative methods; in the pragmatic paradigm the choice of methods, logic and epistemology depends on the research question and 'what works'.

Sample

In the qualitative phase, 50 students were surveyed (one third 'international', two thirds UK). In the quantitative phase, students were randomly assigned to their groups by the module tutor, who then re-assigned to ensure that each group contained at least one, sometimes two, international students. There were twenty groups, consisting of five students each.

Phase 1   Qualitative data

Data collection and analysis

The survey data was collected by a business management student for her dissertation (Feasby, 2005) from the same cohort that provided the marks for phase two of this study. The students' responses were analysed using a template-type approach (Robson, 2002: 458).

Findings

Of the students surveyed, 64% said that they enjoyed group work. This proportion was very similar for both home and international students.

The students' comments on language, nationality, ability and personality issues within their groups focused on the importance of similarity. Typical comments on ability included:

> Group work has been the most enjoyable when all group members have had similar abilities and level of understanding.

> People have different standards of work; one member may be A grade another D so may bring marks down for some.

All students who noted ability as a factor felt that having the same level of ability as others within the group made the group more effective.

The most popular comment was on the importance of good communication within the group. One student mentioned 'language barriers' as a reason why groups did not work together well. Another said, 'I found communication with international students difficult'.

A small number of students mentioned nationality as a reason why groups worked, or did not work well, together. Comments included:

> Chinese are lazy.

> English students are never really punctual or approachable. Very few of them are dedicated to group work. Also, some culture discrimination exists.

> Maybe English people can learn … what's going on in the world a little more, so its easier to talk with people from other cultural backgrounds.

> No commitment of local students as they only talk about their night out and hangovers when the group meets.

Respondents who mentioned nationality as a factor in successful group work indicated that mono-national groups were preferable.

Comments on the personality of group members were less clear on the benefits of similarities or differences. Several mentioned 'personality conflicts' as a factor in unsuccessful group work, but did not say whether the conflict was a result of having too many similar or too many different personalities. The importance of friendship within successful groups was frequently noted; comments included:

> If the group bonds on a social level, they will all feel comfortable with who they are working with (and easily express their opinions).

> [Effective groups] have a good laugh with group members because they get on well.

The importance of *equal* levels of participation was as popular a reason for (un)successful group work as 'communication'. Typical comments included,

> [Unsuccessful groups have] different expectations, some just want to pass with bare minimum, others put in 100%.

> I enjoyed working in a group when all the members were committed to the task set and did a fair percentage of the work.

> I feel that the lazy people get a good ride if they are in a good group.

Difference was recognised as a strength in a group, where knowledge and skills were concerned, for example,

> Everyone has different skills, when working together and using these skills the outcome is better than individual – synergy.

> Sparking ideas and discussion – help each other to make sense and bring out ideas through questioning.

Discussion

Differences between group members' first language, nationality, ability and personality were almost unanimously believed to have a negative effect on group performance by the students surveyed. This is explained by similarity-attraction theory; which suggests that people who consider themselves culturally similar tend to be attracted to each other, and have less difficulty communicating with each other than those who see themselves as culturally heterogeneous. What we *notice* as being different is explained by Mannix & Neale (2005: 43) as follows, 'ultimately, the context provides the backdrop for what is noticed and becomes salient and relevant to organisational actors'.

For the students in this study, 'assessment' creates a context in which 'ability' and 'communication skills' are crucially relevant and, therefore, likely to be noticed. How students judge each others' ability and communication skills may depend on certain aspects of their institutional (and wider social) context. For example, where the institutional talk about students commonly revolves around 'international' versus 'home', 'native speaker' versus 'non-native speaker', 'high achiever' versus 'low achiever' or 'lazy' versus 'hard-working', intra-group differences may become exaggerated, resulting in the confident allocation of peers to discrete categories.

Once a category has been noticed and other students (mentally) placed inside it, the members of the 'other' group are generally considered to be more homogenous than 'us', and to be judged as such more quickly and with more confidence. In fact, both 'academic ability' and 'ability to communicate' are continuous, not discrete, qualities. They are also heavily dependent on institutional definitions of ability and communication, as well as being influenced by the design of a specific task. On the other hand, apart from dual nationals, we all have one 'nationality'; and yet the use of this category to explain other categories, such as ability, motivation and communication skills is as suspect as the categories themselves.

Many students commented on the benefits of 'sameness'; specifically – sharing language, nationality, personality, levels of ability and motivation to participate. Where difference was valued (ideas and skills), the source of difference was assumed to be elsewhere, though exactly where was not specified.

Students were wholly negative about free-riding and their explanations for it were also negative. People who did not do their fair share of the group's work were 'lazy', 'not committed' and 'lack[ed] motivation'. It may indeed be that some students are poorly motivated and happy for others to do their work. But it may also be the case that the 'high stakes' nature of assessment at university increases the likelihood of instrumental motivation and can make free-riding a rational choice.

About half the students surveyed said that they enjoyed group work, implying that group work is a good way of learning or of getting good marks. For these students a possible explanation for higher group than individual marks is subject expectancy bias.

Intra-group diversity seems to be both negative and positive for the students surveyed: negative where it is assumed to be a fixed quality of difference and positive where it is assumed to provide a range of ideas for development by the group. Perhaps, as has been suggested, group outcomes are a result of the members' understanding and use of difference within their group, their *perception* of diversity.

Phase 2   Quantitative data

Phase two of the study aims to answer the question: does having higher ability students in the group increase the group mark or does group work drag everyone's marks down? The following hypotheses are tested:

H1   the individual marks of the lowest achieving student in the group are the strongest predictor of the group mark.

H2   the mean of the individual marks of all students in the group is the strongest predictor of the group mark.

H3   the individual marks of the highest achieving student in the group are the strongest predictor of the group mark.

Data analysis

To answer the question 'Is the difference between the mean group-work score of international students and home students significant?' a *t* test of mean difference is run.

Next, the group-work mark of each of the 20 groups is regressed on to a measure of the individual ability (a mean of the marks achieved in three non-group-work assessments undertaken in the same academic year) of the **lowest** achieving student, the **highest** achieving student and the **mean** individual ability of the group. The aim of the three regressions is to determine the best predictor of group marks.

Finally, the mean mark of the assessed mixed nationality groups is compared with individual mean marks on non-group assessments.

Findings

Differences between home and international students

Having chosen assessment tasks where the students were randomly allocated into multi-national groups, I expected to find very little difference between the average marks of the home and international students. Indeed, the average group-work mark for home students was 58.16% and for international students 56.03%. This differ-ence is statistically insignificant.

In contrast, the marks for the average of three individual assessments do show a statistically significant difference between the average for home students (56.6%), and the average for international students (48.2%).

Correlations

The Pearson product-moment correlation coefficients are insignificant between the average group mark and the lowest individual mark in the group, and positive and significant between the average individual mark ($r = .401$) and the highest individual mark ($r = .634$).

Table 2 Regressions ($N = 100$)

Hypothesis	Mean square of residuals	Standardised beta coefficient	t	sig.	r2
1 (lowest)	77.67	-.024	-.235	.815	.001
2 (mean)	65.23	.401	4.330	.000	.161
3 (highest)	46.49	.634	8.113	.000	.402

The table above shows that the estimated beta coefficients for the lowest achieving students in the group are insignificant at the customary confidence level. This sug-gests that the individual ability of the least able group member is uncorrelated with the performance of the group. H1 can be rejected.

In contrast, the estimated beta coefficients for the relationship between the aver-age group achievement, and the group member with the highest ability do seem to be significant predictors of group performance. The higher the individual mark of the most able student, therefore, the higher the group mark. In fact, the results suggest that for every extra 1% in the individual mark of the best student in the group, the mark of the whole group is expected to rise by 0.63%. H3 can be accepted, as the mark of the strongest individual is the best predictor of the overall group mark.

t tests

The mean mark of the assessed mixed nationality groups (57) is four marks higher than the mean of the non-group assessments (53); this is a statistically significant difference. This result suggests that, in this sample, many of the mixed nationality groups perform at the same, or at a higher level, than the average ability of the individuals that make up the group.

To investigate the relationship between individual and group marks more closely, a paired samples t test to measure the significance of the difference between the group mark and the lowest, mean and highest individual marks was conducted. The difference between the mean group mark (57) and the mean highest individual mark (65) was –7, t (99) = –10.43, p < .05. Between the mean group mark (57) and a mean of the mean individual marks (53), the difference (4) is statistically significant, and the smallest of the three differences, t (99) = 4.32, p < .05. The largest of the three differences, that between the mean group mark (57) and the mean lowest individual mark (44), was 13, t (99) = 12.83, p = < .05.

Discussion

As expected, the differences in the *group* work marks of international and home students were statistically insignificant. However, generally, international students did less well than home students on the *individually* assessed components. As the groups were awarded a group mark for their presentation and report, we are not able to judge whether the international students were thought by the markers to have made a greater or lesser contribution than the home students.

In the second stage of the analysis, we saw that within a group, low and averagely achieving students tend to benefit from being placed in a group with stronger students. Low achieving students stand to gain 13 marks on a group assignment, compared to their mean individual assignment marks. Averagely achieving students gain four marks on group assignments, compared to their mean individual assignment marks. The highest achieving students in the group, however, are disadvantaged by being in a mixed ability group, losing seven marks from their mean individual assignment mark.

These highest achieving students are not necessarily high achievers *per se*; they are the highest achievers in a mixed ability group. They seem to miss out on the opportunity to have their own marks 'dragged up' by even stronger students. This finding is in contrast to a study conducted by De Vita (2002), who found that mixed nationality group marks were as high, or higher, than the average individual mark of the best group member. My results show that the students' fear that group work can have a detrimental effect on their marks is unfounded for the lowest achieving and averagely achieving members; their marks are, in fact, dragged up by group work. The highest achieving students, however, are right to dislike group work. Group work drags the mean mark of the cohort up, but at the expense of the highest achieving individuals in the groups.

The results of the regression suggest that, despite the *t* tests showing that group work drags the mean mark of the cohort up, at the expense of the highest achieving individuals, we cannot be over-confident about the importance of this finding. The value of the coefficient of determination in the highest achieving students' model (R^2 = .402) suggests that although *some* part of the total variation in group-work marks is explained by this model, there are other factors that go beyond the individual ability of the highest achieving member of the group. Group-work marks can be partly explained by the ability of the highest achieving group member, but there are other possible factors that contribute to a complete explanation. This study does not identify or measure any of these other factors and further research is needed to suggest what they might be.

We can only speculate on why some students benefit from group work and others do not. Any, or a combination, of the following reasons may explain the result:

o an information processing effect (pooling resources)
o free-riding on the highest achieving students
o subject or observer expectancy bias.

There does not seem to be a teaching effect, where the highest achieving students benefit from helping those of lower ability than themselves to learn. Neither does there seem to be a synergistic effect, where students work together to produce an outcome that is better than that they could have achieved as individuals. It seems more likely that if there is 'pooling' of resources, the pooling is one way; from the highest achiever to the averagely achieving and lowest achieving students, at the expense of the highest achiever. Put another way, the resources of the highest achiever are diluted by the other students in the group.

Finally, it is important to remember that, although some part of the total variation in group-work marks is explained by the efforts of the highest achieving student, there are other factors that are not accounted for. Further investigation of group-work processes is needed in order to identify these factors and how they may interact with each other and with the ability of the group members. To return to the analysis of the qualitative data in phase one of this study, the importance of ability in mixed nationality groups may depend on other differences that group members notice and ascribe importance to. Which differences these are may depend, in turn, on institutional context, task type and time.

Suggestions for changes in the organisation of mixed-nationality group work

o When setting a group work task, be positive about the benefits of group work, its importance as a useful skill in the work place and as an effective way of learning.
o Design group tasks to require diverse opinions, experiences and skills.
o Assign students to groups so that a range of abilities and other differences are represented. In particular, consider equal distribution of higher achieving students.
o Consider how the group processes, as well as the final product, might be assessed.
o Facilitate agreement from the beginning on the nature of the task.
o Create an atmosphere in which different viewpoints are welcomed by the team.
o Find ways to help diverse team members identify common goals and values.
o Support the views held by the smallest number of people in the team.

o Try to avoid one group member being seen as 'in a minority' – more diversity is better than less.
o Provide training for students in skills for effective group work.

This study has found that many students do benefit from group work, including mixed nationality group work. Exactly how these benefits occur, and why and when they cease to occur for higher achieving students, remains to be seen.

References

De Vita, G. (2002) Does assessed multicultural group work really pull UK students' average down? *Assessment and Evaluation in Higher Education* 27 (2) 153–231

Dight, C. (2007) Diversity. *The Times, Career* 28 June p 12

Ding, W. and Lehrer, S. F. (2005) *Do peers affect student achievement in China's secondary schools?* Available from: http://post.queensu.ca/~dingw/peer.pdf (accessed 27 June 2007)

Feasby, L. (2005) *What are the benefits of group work to undergraduates?* Unpublished BA (Hons) Special Study York: York St John College

Ford, E. (2007) Collaborative working: teamwork gets results. *The Times, Career* 28 June p 12

Hoxby, C. (2000) Peer effects in the classroom: learning from gender and race variation. *NBER Working Papers 7867* National Bureau of Economic Research Inc. Available from http://ideas.repec.org/p/nbr/nberwo/7867.html (accessed 27 June 2007)

Mannix, E. and Neale, M. A. (2005) What differences make a difference? The promise and reality of diverse teams in organizations. *Psychological science in the public interest, American Psychological Society* 6 (2) Available from http://www.blackwell-synergy.com/doi/pdf (last accessed on 27 June 2007)

Pitt, M. J. (2000) The application of games theory to group project assessment. *Teaching in Higher Education* 5 (2) 233–41

Robson, C. (2002) *Real World Research*. Oxford: Blackwell

Tashakkori, A. and Teddlie, C. (1998) *Mixed Methodology: combining qualitative and quantitative approaches*. Thousand Oaks CA: Sage

RACHEL WICAKSONO has taught English, trained teachers and managed schools in the UK, Indonesia, Hong Kong, India, Sri Lanka, Japan, Pakistan, Vietnam, Malaysia and Singapore. She is a senior lecturer at York St John University (YSJU) and head of programme for the YSJU MA Teaching English to Speakers of Other Languages. Her research interests are in the assessment of 'international' students in UK universities, mixed nationality pair and group work, the use of English as an international language and the allocation of resources in Higher Education. She is a freelance writer and broadcaster for the BBC World Service *Learning English* website.

11

Listening to international students

Philip Warwick
York Management School

Listening to customers is a good principle in marketing. When taught masters students were asked about their teaching and learning experience, the opinions of a cohort of largely international students identified several issues, leading to significant change.

Introduction

An annual student survey focused on teaching and learning can help programme leaders make incremental changes to their programme. This type of approach is particularly suited to a one-year taught masters programme. By repeating the survey, it is relatively easy to judge how effective changes have been and this approach can quickly build into a longitudinal survey, illustrating how student perceptions vary over the years.

The York Management School (TYMS) became aware of the needs of a diverse, largely international, student population as a result of conducting an annual *Listening to Masters Students Survey*. It is anticipated that the annual round of survey, review and incremental change is likely to continue for some time to come.

Objectives

The aim of this project was to survey a largely international student cohort so that the staff at TYMS could learn from the students' experiences, and find ways to improve the programme and others like it in the future.

The following specific objectives were identified for the *Listening to Masters Students* project:

○ To engage international, EU and home students in a dialogue about their learning experiences during the second term of their one year masters programme.
○ To review the programme in the light of the research findings.
○ To disseminate the understanding gained from this project to other departments around the university.
○ To use the survey as a basis for a longitudinal study to determine if changes to the programme led to greater student satisfaction.

Rationale

The research strategy adopted by the project team used a mixture of inductive and deductive approaches to gather student views. In year one, two temporary research assistants (both international PhD students), conducted loosely structured interviews with 25% of the students. Four focus groups were arranged, covering a further 25% of the cohort, to discuss the main issues that arose from interviewing individuals. Finally, the views of the whole group were captured by a short questionnaire. The questionnaire (Table 1) was given out at the end of the second term and repeated in 2006–07 and 2007–08.

At the end of the second term, students who had completed all their taught modules were about to embark on their dissertations. The questionnaire covered the following issues:

Induction
Did it provide the student with the information, skills and knowledge they needed to start the programme?

Assessment
Were the assessment formats what they were expecting?

Teaching styles
Did students prefer lectures, seminars or group work?

Working with others
How did they find working in groups?

Workload
Was the workload too onerous?

English language
Did the international students improve their English while studying in the UK?

Overall satisfaction
Would students recommend studying at York to friends?

In order to make the questionnaire as relevant as possible (and to overcome problems of evaluation fatigue) it was given out during a dissertation-preparation workshop, in which students were not only asked to fill in the questionnaire but later in the session they were asked to critique the questionnaire and the survey methods. The completed survey rate varied as follows: 65% in 2005–06, 46% in 2006–07 and 76% in 2007–08.

In addition to the questionnaire, three student focus groups (one of home students, one EU and one of Chinese and Taiwanese students) were arranged in 2007–08 to discuss the results.

An action research approach was adopted from the start (Saunders et al, 2003) with adjustments made to the programme in response to each survey. Outcomes were reviewed subsequently using the following year's survey as a measure of success.

Table 1   Listening to masters students questionnaire

Induction and pre-course information

1 I had all the information I needed before I came to York.
2 I had enough information about the workload and class size.
3 I understood what assessments I would have to do before I arrived.
4 The induction programme gave a useful introduction to studying in York.

Teaching and learning

5 I preferred the lectures where the lecturer talked for the whole session.
6 I preferred lectures where the class discussed questions.
7 I preferred doing group work with colleagues rather than the lectures.
8 I preferred seminars when the class was split into smaller groups.
9 I was able to understand and follow lectures.
10 Have you any general comments about the teaching on the course?

Group work/Study groups

11 I preferred to work on my own rather than do study group exercises.
12 I enjoyed doing group works/study group exercises with other students.
13 I found it hard to talk with other students during the group work
14 I learnt a lot from my colleagues when doing the group work.

Workload

15 The workload has been about right.
16 I have had too much work to do. I have not kept up with requirements.

General issues

17 My English language skills have improved while studying at York.
18 I have not used spoken English as much as I wanted to do.
19 How likely is it that you would recommend studying at York to a friend?
20 Are there any reasons why you would not recommend studying at York?

Context

In October 2005, TYMS started a new taught masters programme that attracted a largely international student cohort (see Table 2). At this time, teaching and support staff in the school were not used to working with large culturally diverse groups of home or international students (Warwick, 2007): many faced a very steep learning curve. The action-research project was seen as one way to evaluate the outcome and learn from the experience.

Description
Survey results

Several interesting themes emerged from the survey results. This paper concentrates on teaching styles and student workload, on working with other students, use of English, the induction arrangements and assessment tasks.

Teaching styles

In 2005–06 the one-to-one interviews suggested that students liked clear speaking, well-structured sessions, useful handouts, etc. Students in the focus groups were more critical of teaching styles. The 2005–06 students said they were unhappy with

Table 2   York University, taught masters programme student numbers

Origins	2005–06	2006–07	2007–08
Home	3	7	9
European Union (EU)	13	6	10
Chinese	93	51	65
Other international	15	5	12
Total	124	69	96

staff who did not allow time for questions at the end of sessions and those who were not available in the school or who did not answer emails.

In 2005–06, the majority of modules were timetabled and taught in two-hour lecture slots. Perhaps as a result, the 2005–06 questionnaire identified considerable dissatisfaction that most teaching was done in large groups with much less small group work than students had expected to encounter on a UK-based masters programme. In 2006–07 and 2007–08, once seminars and group work became a routine part of the programme, responses to the statement 'I preferred doing group work ... to lectures' changed from clear support in 2005–06 (40% in favour, 23% against) to a slight preference in 2008 (38% for, 36% against).

Even more noticeable were the answers to the seminar-group question. In 2005–06, 72% said they wanted the class broken down into smaller groups but this figure had dropped to 53% in 2007–08, perhaps because this had been a daily occurrence on their programme. Responses to questions on class discussions show less interest in class discussions in 2007–08 than in the two previous years (41% said they liked sessions where the classed discussed questions, compared with 48% in 2005–06 and 2006–07). The 2007–08 focus groups revealed that home students were the least happy discussing issues in seminars (they preferred lectures).

The questions about understanding lectures did show a marginal improvement over the three years. In 2005–06, 54% said they could understand lectures, while 16% said were not able to understand. By 2007–08, 64% of the students said they were able to understand lectures although worryingly, 14% still said they could not understand the content of lectures.

Workload

Given the figures for understanding lectures, it is not unexpected that the questions about workload also led to a mixed response. In the interviews and focus-group meetings in 2005–06, there was near universal agreement that students had had to work extremely hard to complete the required reading, prepare work for the next week's lectures and any assessments, with some students estimating that they were working for 18 hours per day on their studies.

Many of the East Asian students on the programme indicated that language problems meant that they spent long hours getting through the required reading.

However the questionnaire results painted a different picture; 38% of the 2005–06 students indicated that they had not had too much work to do and 30% agreed with the statement 'the workload has been about right'. These responses seem to indicate that although many of the 2005–06 class had to work extremely hard and felt under intense pressure, around a third of the cohort had no difficulty keeping up with the workload.

The 2007–08 students answered in a similar way with a significant spread of answers: 45% suggested that they had too much to do, 32% thought the workload is about right, the rest gave neutral answers. The 2007–08 focus groups reflected this range of views. The EU student focus group seemed the least concerned about workload pressures.

Working with others

The 2005–06 student interviews and focus groups provided a range of views about group work and working with other students.

- Some clearly indicated that they did not like group work and that they avoided taking an active part in it.
- Some did not feel they should be asked to do group work as part of a lesson, while others indicated that they liked working with others.
- Some enjoyed working with fellow nationals, while others enjoyed meeting and working with people from other nations and cultures.

These different opinions carried through into the questionnaire. Nevertheless, in 2005–06 group work exercises seemed to be popular overall, 59% of student agreed with the statement 'I enjoyed doing group work exercises with other students'.

In contrast the 2007–08 group seemed more orientated to working on their own, 37% saying they preferred working on their own and less than half – 46% – saying they enjoyed doing group work. Only 29% of the 2007–08 group felt they had 'learnt a lot from my colleagues'. In the 2007–08 focus groups the home students were the least satisfied with their group work experiences, while the EU and Chinese students appeared much more enthusiastic.

Use of English

In 2005–06 many East Asian and European students were concerned and disappointed that there were so many Mandarin-speaking students, so that 70% agreed with the statement 'I have not used spoken English as much as I wanted to'. In that first year, only 40% agreed with the statement, 'My English skills have improved while studying at York'. The 2006–07 and 2007–08 students' responses to these questions did show a significant improvement, so that by 2007–08, 70% felt their English had improved while studying at York. There is of course still much room for improvement.

Induction

Induction arrangements are vital for one-year masters programmes because students have so little time to adjust to studying at a new level often in a new country. The questionnaire results show a gradual improvement in the response to induction but there are still some problems to overcome. In 2005–06, 63% of the group said they did not have enough information about workload and class size before they arrived in York. This figure fell to 28% in 2007/2008. Despite a significant effort to improve the induction programme over the last two years, 18% in 2006–07 group and 16% of in 2007–08 still said the induction programme was not useful to them.

Assessment

Detailed questions about module-assessment strategies are posed in individual module evaluations; this survey placed the emphasis on prior expectations of assessment. In the interview and focus groups in 2005–06, students were mainly concerned with the time available to complete exams and to write assignments. They said that time pressures meant that they adopted strategies based on coping rather than doing their best work. In the questionnaire students were asked about expectations of assessment. Many students said that they did not understand what type of assessment to expect before starting the course. This figure has remained fairly constant over three years at around 40%.

Overall satisfaction

The final question in the questionnaire survey was essentially marketing research. In service industries it is generally held that there is a very strong link between an organisation's success and the proportion of customers who are 'promoters' of the service (Reichheld, 2003). Promoters are those people who are most likely to give a word-of-mouth recommendation for the product or service. The questionnaire asked: 'How likely is it that you would recommend studying at York to a friend?' (Question 19).

The responses were used to calculate the net promoter figure by excluding the neutrals and undecided to leave a figure for those would recommend minus those who would not. The net approval rating was 59% for 2007–08, compared to 42% for 2006–07 and 10% for 2005–06. The school is pleased that the net promoter figure has improved over the three surveys. However, Amazon and Ebay, the most successful companies Reichheld studied at the start of the current decade, achieved net promoter figures of around 75%, so there is still some distance to go.

Action taken as a result of the survey

For the last three years the survey results have helped the programme director and staff teaching on the programme to identify issues concerning significant numbers of students on the programme. Action has been taken in the following areas:

Recruitment and expectations management

In response to feedback on workload, a clearer separation between the students on the MSc Management with Business Finance and those on the MA in Management has allowed for both more optional modules and less pressure at the end of the first term.

There is little point in admitting students who are likely to fail the programme because of poor language skills. The problems faced by some students have led to more detailed scrutiny of IELTS scores to ensure no components of the score fall below 6.0 and the creation of an alternative entry route for students with IELTS score of 6.0. These students can choose to attend a two-month summer school in York prior to beginning their studies. Results for these students clearly indicate that they perform as well, if not better, than those students entering with an IELTS score of 6.5 (Soden and Warwick, 2008). All international students are encouraged to attend *English for academic purposes* support in the first term.

Over the summer months, a monthly newsletter is sent out to all students who have been offered a place providing them with information about assessment methods, preparatory reading, likely workload, module choices, social events and staff activities.

Induction processes

The importance of induction is referred to in the literature (Turner and Acker, 2002; Carroll and Ryan, 2005) as well as being an issue in the survey. Drip-feeding the most important information at appropriate moments is the recommended approach (Ladd and Ruby, 1999; Wisker, 2003; Gannon-Leary and Smailes, 2004). In 2007–08, induction was spread out over an extended period. Talks about preparation for assessment and academic misconduct take place in the second half of the first term, at a point where they are more relevant and less abstract. In an attempt to improve group work, additional social space and a team-building exercise were introduced in the 2007–08 induction programme, with more emphasis laid on getting to know each other.

Group work

To facilitate group work in 2006–07 and 2007–08, students were arranged in a series of multi-national and multi-cultural study groups. In 2006 the groups were mainly designed to act as peer-support groups and were not particularly effective. In 2007–08 students attended seminars in their study groups and most modules leaders used study groups as the basis for case study preparation between sessions. Wherever possible the tasks assigned to the groups have an international theme, requiring home students to take an international perspective while at the same time avoiding putting international students at a disadvantage (De Vita, 2001; Carroll and Ryan, 2005).

It is interesting to note that, as group work has become a more onerous requirement of the programme rather than an occasional treat, students have become less enthusiastic about doing it. Discussion in the 2007–08 focus groups identified that it was the home students who are the most sceptical about the benefits of working with their colleagues (Leki, 2001 and Parks & Raymond, 2004 refer to this type of home-student scepticism).

Access to staff and supervision

As a result of the survey of 2005–06 survey students all staff set up four hours per week of office hours. Staff were also encouraged to allow time at the end of lectures for students to ask informal questions. Access to staff has not been raised as an issue in 2006–07 or 2007–08, suggesting this action has been effective.

Teaching and learning strategies

The majority of the 2005–06 students said they preferred smaller groups, indicating dissatisfaction with the prevailing class size. To overcome this problem, classes were broken down into smaller seminar sessions whenever practicable. The standard teaching model was changed from a two-hour lecture slot to one-hour lectures supported by weekly seminars in smaller groups. Responses to the 2007–08 survey suggest that as with group work, students are less keen to attend seminars when they become a routine requirement of the programme.

In 2005–06, students said they liked staff to provide a clear structure for modules and for each lecture. They wanted staff to deliver material at an even pace, not speeding through lectures. This message was passed on to staff who have been encouraged through their module-evaluation reports to reflect on the adaptations they have made to their modules to accommodate the international student population. Comments made by students in 2007–08 suggest that most staff have adapted their teaching over the last three years. It would be incorrect to say that all lectures by all staff are well received. However, student experiences seem to be improving and staff continue to learn from their teaching experiences.

Many international students have a limited vocabulary (Carroll and Ryan, 2005) so many find it hard to work with complicated academic language both in lectures and when receiving feedback and assessment instructions. Staff are encouraged to avoid using unexplained metaphors, to explain technical language and above all to use straightforward language in assessment questions and exam papers. The management school has a peer-review mechanism in the assessment process. As part of this, colleagues are now asked to review questions for any language or contextual understanding that would inadvertently penalise international students (Hayes and Introna, 2003).

Assessment and workload

The timing of assessments and the uneven distribution of workload that this implies have been a concern for around a third of students in all three surveys. In the 2007–08 focus groups the home students and Chinese students said they were concerned about assessment workload. In an effort to reduce the pressure, hand-in dates and exams have been spread out towards the end of the 2007–08 programme, but more needs to be done on this issue and it is a priority for action in 2008–09.

Evaluation

The information provided by the annual survey served to focus attention on specific teaching and learning issues. Following discussion among staff teaching the programme, it has been possible to agree actions to address specific teaching and learning issues. Some, but not all, changes have had a beneficial effect on student satisfaction. The 2007–08 response to group working is a good example of an unexpected adverse outcome.

Discussion

A range of formal quality-assurance systems have worked alongside the listening project survey described above. These include computerised individual module evaluations, a staff–student liaison committee and student representation on formal departmental committees. However for the last three years, the most useful programme specific information has come from this annual listening survey. Changes made to the programme – the introduction of seminars, changes to the assessment timetable, the organisation of group work, changes to induction and entry requirements and even the adoption of an office-hours system in 2006–07 – all result from listening to student feedback and making small incremental changes to the programme.

Coupling the survey with an action-research approach means that it is relatively easy to identify an issue, make appropriate changes and then measure the impact of the changes. There have been some significant and successful improvements, such as the improvements to the amount of English used by international students and the impact of a range of changes on the net promoter figure.

However, not all changes have been well received and there remains much work to be done. The teaching styles and workload responses suggest that language ability remains an issue for international students (Warwick, 2007). The evidence seems to suggest that students with the weakest language skills are still struggling to understand lectures and keep up with coursework. Exacerbating the difficulties these students face, it seems that home students and others with better language skills are increasingly intolerant of those who they feel are not contributing to the programme.

Similarly, group-working arrangements continue to be an issue. Teaching staff feel that group work is an important component of a management masters programme (De Vita, 2001; Kaye and Hawkridge, 2003). Flowerdew (1998) emphasises that group work is particularly suitable as an approach to learning for students from

Chinese cultural backgrounds; home and EU students are generally well used to group work. However, this does not mean that group work is going to be successful for all students in all situations. Despite the introduction of team-building work and clear explanations in the induction programme about why TYMS believes in the need and usefulness of multi-cultural group work over half the students in 2007–08 said they did not enjoy doing group work exercises. Volet and Ang (1998), Ho et al (2004) and Cathcart et al (2006) all noted problems in the relationships between home and East Asian international students. It seems that inter-student relationships during group work continue to cause problems at York and will need further attention in the coming years.

Staff reactions to internationalisation were considered by Turner (2006). She suggested that not all internationalisation initiatives, changes and modifications are going to be universally adopted and implemented willingly by staff. At York, a lot of changes have been introduced over the last three years. Perhaps the shock of such a radical change in the number of international students in the School (from 12 in 2002–03, to 214 five years later in 2007–08), has led to a willingness to effect changes. A more gradual change in international student numbers might not have had the same impact. A collective will to improve the programme following a very difficult first year has meant that teaching staff have been prepared to reflect on their teaching and learning experiences (Fry et al, 1999; Turner, 2006) and listen and respond to the student viewpoint.

Much work remains to be done but we hope that the continued use of the action research approach discussed in this chapter will allow for ongoing incremental changes.

References

Carroll, J. and Ryan, J. (2005) eds *Teaching international students improving learning for all.* Abingdon: Routledge

Cathcart, A., Dixon-Dawson, J. and Hall, R. (2006) Reluctant Hosts and disappointed guests? Examining expectations and enhancing experiences of cross cultural group work in postgraduate business programmes. *International Journal of Management Education* 5 (1) p 13–22

De Vita, G. (2001) The use of group work in large and diverse business management classes some critical issues. *International Journal of Management Education* 1 (3) pp 27–35

Flowerdew, L. (1998) A cultural perspective on group work. *ELT Journal* 52 (4) pp 323–29

Fry, H. Ketteridge, S. and Marshall, S. (1999) *A handbook for teaching and learning in Higher Education, enhancing academic practice.* London: Kogan Page

Gannon-Leary, P. and Smailes, J. (2004) Diverse student needs: the challenge for teaching international students. Paper presented at Business Education Support Team Conference, Edinburgh 2004

Hayes, N. and Introna, L. (2003) *Alienation and plagiarism: coping with otherness in assessment practice.* Lancaster Management School Working Paper 2003–094

Ho, E., Holmes, P. and Cooper, J. (2004) *Review and evaluation of international literature on managing cultural diversity in the classroom.* Wellington NZ: Ministry of Education.

Kaye, R. and Hawkridge, D. (2003) *Learning and Teaching for Business, case studies of successful innovation*. London: Kogan Page

Ladd, P. and Ruby, R. (1999) Learning Styles adjustment issues of International students. *Journal of Education for Business* **74** (6) pp 363–368

Leki, I. (2001) A narrow thinking system: non-native English Speaking Students in group projects across the curriculum. *TESOL Quarterly* **35** (1) pp 39–66

Parks, S. and Raymond, P. (2004) Strategy use by non-native English speaking students in an MBA programme: not Business as Usual! *The Modern Language Journal* **88** (3) pp 374–89

Reichheld, F. (2003) The one number you need to grow. *Harvard Business Review* December 2003 pp 46–54

Saunders, M., Lewis, P. and Thornhill, A. (2003) *Research methods for business students*. Harlow, Pearson Education

Soden, W. and Warwick, P. (2008) English Language Entry Requirements for the Taught Masters in Management. Unpublished report, University of York

Turner, Y. and Acker, A. (2002) *Education in the New China*. Aldershot: Ashgate

Turner, Y. (2006) Academic development for intercultural competence: mapping tensions between compliance and commitment. Paper presented at 11th Annual SEDA conference. Birmingham, November 2006

Volet, S. and Ang, D. (1998) Culturally mixed groups on international campuses. *Higher Education Research and Development* **17** (1) pp 5–23

Warwick, P. (2007) Well meant but misguided, an attempt to support overseas management studies students in the UK. *International Journal of Management Education* **6** (2) p 3–17

Wisker, G. (2003) Hanging on in there a long way from home. *Educational Developments* **4** (4) p 21–3

PHILIP WARWICK has worked at the York Management School since 2003, teaching on a range of programmes from first-year undergraduate to post-experience masters programmes. He is currently head of the school's taught masters programmes.

Since 2003, he has pursued an interest in teaching international students and has several publications in this field. In 2005–06, he was awarded a university teaching fellowship grant to visit universities in New Zealand and Australia to study their approach to teaching international students. He is currently working towards a PhD on the theme of the internationalising of higher education.

12

Reflective practice and learning styles with international students

Jacqueline Lynch
University of Westminster

The case study illustrates how a postgraduate marketing module
develops reflective practice with international students and
explores how much learning styles influence that ability.

Context/rationale

The *Global Marketing Strategies* module is part of the MA Global Business degree, at the University of Westminster Business School. The masters programme is run with international partners in France, Germany, Spain, and Russia. On average, there are 20 students in each of the European institutions who study the module, with lower numbers in Russia as the institution is establishing itself and the programme.

Students come to the UK to study the masters programme from all over the world – Europe, Asia, South America, North America, the Middle East and Australia. As part of the higher education (HE) policy of developing personal development plans (PDPs) and transferable skills, students were asked to reflect on their learning at different points throughout the module.

Reflection and PDPs are not concepts to which many international students are accustomed. There are also cultural stereotypes attached to the ability of international students to reflect. When teaching on the module began students did not immediately understand what 'reflection' meant, were not sure what was required of them, and were apprehensive about sharing personal reflection.

The aim of the study was to introduce, practise and improve reflection as part of the learning experience and ultimately, to incorporate this into the PDP. Students were given the opportunity to practise reflection at key points in the module both as individuals and as a group and were given appropriate feedback. At the end of the module students prepared a reflective statement on learning as part of a group project which was assessed.

Reflective learning is also important in postgraduate programmes because it is combined with taught and research elements (Bourner, 2003). Initially, reflection was introduced within the module as a small piece of assessed work with details about what to cover and the assessment criteria, with some explanation. The resulting reflective statements were adequate but there was concern about the level of critical analysis.

After much thought and reading the literature from key authors, over the years staff have incorporated new ideas into the approach, which has had a marked improvement in the students' ability to reflect:

○ Developing the capacity to reflect (Barnett, 1995)
○ Reflective practitioners (Schon, 1983) and experiential learning (Kolb, 1984)
○ Measures of reflection (Costa and Garmston, 1994) e.g. taxonomies, critical incidents, portfolios, dialogues and interviews
○ Assessing reflective learning (Bourner, 2003) who suggests that
    the key to developing reflective learners is developing a repertoire of reflective questions and providing opportunities to practise them.
○ With appropriate practice and time students can reflect and engage in 'double loop' learning (Leithwood & Steinbach, 1992 cited in Barnett, 1995).
○ Because reflection is a cognitive skill students can improve their reflective capability if they practise and are given appropriate feedback (Barnett, 1995).

Whichever standpoint you take, reflective learning is becoming increasingly important.

Aims

This case study looked at the student learning experience of using reflective practice both as a formative and summative assessed component in a postgraduate module with international students.

Objectives

○ To understand and explore international students' cultural issues which may affect their ability to use reflection as part of their learning experience.
○ To examine the relationship between personal learning style and the students' level of engagement with reflective practice.

The exploratory research was used in the case study and adopted an action-research approach using quantitative and qualitative instruments. Data was collected via observations and discussion in class. Interviews were carried out at the end of the module and an analysis of the reflective statements was undertaken. Students were also contacted several months later to explore whether reflective practice had been embedded into other learning situations. Data from the university questionnaire was also used to gain a fuller picture.

The approach

During induction week, students are introduced to the programme and the major elements that they will have to tackle. In particular a number of key concepts are introduced to them, for example: PDP, cross-cultural learning, reflection and exercises in team building and team bonding.

When the module was first run some years ago, students were asked to reflect without staff actually defining it or explaining it in any great detail. However, the term 'reflective practice' has become popular and with that, problematic, as the interpretation of the term has become very diverse and may be difficult for students to grasp (Morrison, 1996). To overcome these issues the teaching team introduced students to two ideas – Kolb's experiential learning cycle (Kolb, 1984) and Schon's notion of the reflective practitioner (Schon, 1983).

Within the module, the concept of reflection was defined and explained in the first teaching week and reiterated throughout the module. As previously observed, reflection is considered to be a cognitive skill and the expectation is that with practice this skill will improve (Barnett, 1995). With practice and time students can engage in double-loop learning (Leithwood and Steinbach, 1992).

Students were asked to reflect at various points within the module and record their thoughts and ideas to practise the skill so that this would help them to write their final reflective statement. Students were also asked to consider their progression and development throughout the module and to use the examples and critical incidents recorded to improve their learning. They were encouraged to capture the information as part of their online PDP.

In summary, students were allowed to practise reflection in several different ways, from individual private reflection to peer assessment and comments in group exercises. They were asked to record:

○ Observations about peer presentations in class – comments about what aspect were weaker and where the presentation could be improved.
○ Individual reflection in class, which students were then asked to share aloud in class (Lee and Barnett, 1994). Using this idea students were then asked to expand and extend discussion with more searching questions.
○ Their learning as a result of a poster presentation and discussion in class. They were given a week to reflect and record their comments. This was carried out on an individual basis.
○ Significant events from working in groups on their assignment. This could be from any angle that was pertinent to them, for example, either skills or theoretical understanding. In this way they could record an improvement in their understanding of marketing theory or its application, or team skills, dealing with frustration, negotiation and overcoming issues.
○ Formative assessment of individual written reflections halfway through the module where feedback was given but no marks awarded. The emphasis here

was on learning and not assessment.

○ Written reflective statements about learning from a team situation which were assessed and marks awarded.

In terms of learning styles, these were discussed generally and with each student.

Measuring reflection

Costa and Garmston (1994) refer to ways of measuring reflection. One way is by verbal statements expressed in dialogues and interviews, which can capture current thinking. Written reflections can be captured in portfolios and will show progression in learning, for example. It is particularly important that we have a shared under-standing across the partner institutions and teaching teams of how reflection will be assessed.

Just as there were many opportunities to practise reflection there were an equal number of opportunities to receive feedback. The feedback was not confined to the lecturers, as probing questions also came from the students themselves.

The culmination of the approach for the module was the production of a reflective statement about the learning that had taken place within the module. This could be from an academic-content stance, skills-development or individual-development point of view. Students were asked to write a critical reflection and not just merely a description of the process.

Students were assessed in response to using a set of four questions to elicit reflec-tive thoughts:

○ What you have learned about your strengths and weaknesses?
○ What you have learned as a member of the team?
○ What would you do differently as a result of the team experience?
○ How do you think you apply the learning from this experience to your working life?

Evidence of effectiveness

Main findings

In the first few years of using reflection on the module, students from China and some other parts of south-east Asia found the task particularly daunting, with an overriding tendency to 'write what they thought I wanted to hear', or to describe the process, or to reflect on how wonderful the lecturer was. They were not alone as other nationalities (those from India) displayed similar reactions.

From the data that has been collected over the years a number of themes have emerged – feelings about the use of reflection, the formality of reflection and appro-priate language, whether reflection should be assessed, issues concerning timing, dif-ferent learning approaches, the friendliness of professors and cultural development.

Feelings about reflection

Many students were initially apprehensive about reflection but this was not linked to any one nationality. While it was evident there may be cultural issues at play, there are also other factors such as prior learning experience and possibly the influence of the personality of the student.

Feelings about reflection

'My initial reaction – Ha ha, she must be joking! Then the panic started. What am I supposed to write? ... I am not sure what to write ... it was difficult for me.' (female 24 Malaysia)

'It was odd and a bit unsettling for me. I felt uncomfortable. Usually it is required to write down and apply things we have learned before. But in this case it was very difficult to write down the plain truth...' (male 36 Germany)

'I feel nervous.' (female 24 China)

'Sometimes it is hard to put into words what exactly you think. I wasn't afraid but a bit nervous.' (female 25 Turkey)

Formality and language

Students were asked about reflection in terms of giving a view versus writing their thoughts down.

Formality of reflection

Written reflection

'I prefer to do it in writing, I'm better at expressing myself through writing.' (female 24 Malaysia)

'I felt concerned about writing it down... and about what the teacher wanted to see...you cannot really tell the truth.' (male 25 Argentina)

'I didn't feel very free or easy to do reflection, because in my country it is very different. We don't do reflection in such a formal way.' (male 24 Pakistan)

Informal reflection

'If it involves speaking out with lecturers or peers I will not be confident.' (female 24 Malaysia)

'I would prefer to use reflection informally.' (male 36 Germany)

'I like to discuss what I learned with my friends and class mates in a friendly manner open to all thoughts.' (male 24 Pakistan)

'However, it is difficult for me to communicate with members of the team caused by different accents as everyone is from different country with different first language. As well as it is not easy for them to understand what I said.' (female 23 China)

Some students preferred to talk about their reflection, whilst others preferred to write it down. This may be related to their command of English, where some students felt their written English was better than their spoken English. It was also linked to the personal nature of what was being written and the implication that students felt there may be some form of 'judgement' either personally or about the mark.

Assessment of written reflection

Students felt that reflection should not be assessed, as it was too personal to be marked. As mentioned above, there was also a tendency for some students to try to be strategic in their approach by writing what would earn them a good mark rather than an assessment of themselves. This may be linked to cultural issues of not admitting that they are not 'good' at certain tasks or that their skills need to be improved.

Assessing reflection

'...it's always the opportunity for you to 'add' and exaggerate ...to acknowledge that you have learned something to get better grades!' (female 24 Malaysia)

'Despite the fact that I got a good mark for my written statement, I think reflective statements should not be assessed.' (male 36 Germany)

'Taking it into account that we were going to be evaluated on the reflection, my first thought was what do I have to write in order to get a decent mark.' (male 25 Argentina)

Students were initially reticent, but once the situation had been explained and they had been allowed time to practise in a 'safe' environment, they engaged positively with the experience.

Timing

'I feel OK, nothing particularly difficult. Just I need time to reflect.' (female 23 Taiwan)

'I could not reflect as fast as others.' (female 25 Turkey)

'On this moment I think it is pretty difficult for me to evaluate my learning experience because I feel I cannot judge something or formulate a complete learning experience at this stage of the programme.' (female 25 Sweden).

Again timing may be linked with language difficulties or perhaps it is simply that reflection takes time. The quotation above illustrates that one student did not really want to evaluate the module at that particular moment and was reticent to give a view until much later on.

Prior learning environment

'The new teaching system is completely different from the Italian system... Here, the professors are always approachable and I see them more like friends than authorities. Usually, we are always involved in challenging discussions and I can really feel the professors being interested in the viewpoints of their students.' (male 25 Italy)

Some of the UK students who were used to the notion of reflection and producing PDPs followed a process and appeared to adopt a rather mechanistic approach. Interestingly, a few international students who had been studying in the UK for their first degree and had prior experience of reflection demonstrated similar tendencies.

The place where a student studied for their first degree may have an influence on reflection but no firm conclusions can be drawn from the current data.

Cultural development

There were displays of cultural elements, for example, revering the lecturer and fear of 'losing face', and 'shyness'. However, even within different nationalities differences were highlighted. Some of this depended on where the student had taken their first degree (see below).

The overwhelming learning from the module was about cultural differences and group work where much of the reflection suggested that skills and patience were tested! This was evidenced in the reflective statements.

> 'The individuals that are in our class represent 11 different nations, each with their own unique outlook on marketing, as well as other things. It is extremely interesting to see different perspectives on things, all because of varying backgrounds, cultural differences and experiences.' (male 23 USA).

> 'My experience so far has been extremely useful because I can better manage cultural differences and I am really learning how to work in a multicultural context.' (male 25 Italy, group work comment)

The links with learning styles heightened students' awareness of their differences in terms of approach to studying, especially in group work. It helped students to understand their individual behaviour and those of their peers in the group situation. Some students acknowledged that what they initially saw as 'non-contribution' (for example, a student sitting back and listening) actually proved to be an erroneous assumption. They learned to ask for input from each other rather than just expecting it. The links with learning styles helped students to have a sense of how they learned but as yet there are no conclusive findings that can be linked to reflection. There was evidence of improvement in confidence, be it about an ability to speak up, communicate effectively or to realise that the students' language skills were better than they thought!

Students were re-interviewed a few months later to investigate whether reflective practice had been embedded in other learning situations.

What enabled practice to work

Creating a safe environment for students to practise reflection is critical to success. Practice reduces the barriers and the 'fear'; building trust is also crucial. There were many opportunities and exercises where students could assess what I meant by reflection and we discussed the issues as they arose. Open and clear communication also helped with the activities and with building rapport. The introduction of a formative assessment in which students could write a reflective piece and submit it for feedback produced good results. Finally, the activities take time to develop, and it is therefore imperative that space is created in the lecture timetable to allow the practice to take place.

Challenges faced

The main challenges were to overcome student fear and apprehension and in addition, being clear about assessing and measuring reflection (Costa and Garmston, 1994). It is necessary to allow sufficient time for students to assimilate their learning. Informal reflection was well accepted, but assessed reflection raised more issues.

Post-study research suggests that the students saw the relevance of reflection at the time but may not be using the skills to any great effect in other learning. The challenge is how to capture the learning and not lose its value for the rest of the programme. This is particularly true in the international context and with the partner institutions. Interestingly, the best feedback from students about the process came several years later, particularly in relation to group work.

Lessons learned

The lessons have been through trial and error. In summary:

○ Reflection needs to be defined so that students are clear about its nature. It also helped that the definition was less academic and expressed in a simple context to which students could relate more easily.

○ Practising reflection at many points in the module improved students' ability to reflect – the practice of reflection certainly allows time for students to get used to the approach.

○ Learning styles helped students to understand how they learn and gave them a better sense of 'themselves'. Early explanation of reflection and learning styles in induction week was very productive in setting the scene and allowed the ideas to be developed.

○ A safe environment and trust between students and lecturers is necessary.

○ Knowing their learning style actually helped students to reflect in their group situation.

○ Time needs to be built into the module to achieve the desired results.

○ Working with international partners is a key challenge in itself, with communication carried out at a distance and different approaches to teaching and learning.

○ Shared understanding from the start is crucial in terms of what is acceptable for assessment and grading, for example, superficial reflective statements versus critical reflective statements. This depends on the nature and type of questions staff use, and the probing and practice of what is meant by criticality. Feedback to the students on their development of reflection is very important (Bourner, 2003).

○ The success of reflective practice depends on how often staff practise reflection with students or provide opportunities to reflect and also their own attitudes towards its importance.

○ In addition, linking the learning from the module with PDP and the overall learning environment is essential.

New developments on the module

A number of new initiatives are being discussed by the module team to build on current practice:

○ The introduction of a learning journal to address the issues outlined above.

○ Improved links into the student PDPs both within the module and across the programme.

○ Further activities to encourage skills in reflection, for example, developing reflection aloud so that students can peer-assess each other and develop further questioning techniques (see Lee and Barnett's work, 1994).

○ Staff development via a workshop to share ideas and develop practice at the annual International Business School Alliance (IBSA) conference.

The case study illustrates a very rich picture of the issues that are pertinent when teaching and assessing reflection with international students, the lessons learned and the potential for further development.

References

Barnett, B. (1995) Developing reflection and expertise: can mentors make a difference? *Journal of Educational Administration* **33** (5) pp 45–59

Bourner (2003) Assessing Reflective Learning. *Education and Training* **45** (5) pp 267–72

Costa, A. L. & Garmston, R. J. (1994) *Cognitive coaching: A foundation for renaissance schools.* Berkeley CA: The Institute for Intelligent Behavior

Kolb, G. (1984) *Experiential Learning Experience as the source of Learning and Development.* Englewood Heights NJ: Prentice Hall

Lee, G. V. and Barnett, B. G. (1994) Using reflective questioning to promote collaborative dialogue. *Journal of Staff Development* **15** (1) pp 16–21

Morrison, K. (1996) Developing reflective practice in higher degree students through a learning journal. *Studies in Higher Education* **21** (3) pp 317–32

Schon, D. A. (1983) *The Reflective Practitioner how professionals think in action.* Tavistock: London

JACQUELINE LYNCH is a principal lecturer and subject leader in marketing and became one of the first teaching fellows of the University of Westminster. She is also a chartered marketer and member of the Chartered Institute of Marketing, Institute of Direct Marketing and Higher Education Academy. She has a passion for learning and teaching and her teaching research interests are in feedback to students, managing student expectations, internationalisation of the curriculum, marketing education, graduate employment in marketing, marketing and logistics, and creativity.

13

Critical thinking
Discussion between Chinese postgraduate international students and their lecturers

Rong Huang *Plymouth Business School*
University of Plymouth

Critical thinking is an issue for postgraduates which
can be elusive and is not just cultural. Students and their
lecturers understand the concept differently and international
students need more support in helping to develop it.

The research aim and objectives

This project is an attempt to understand Chinese postgraduate international students' experience of critical thinking during their masters degree in Tourism and Hospitality Management at the University of Plymouth. There are four main objectives:

1 To investigate the students' perceptions of critical thinking.
2 To assess the students' problems in applying critical thinking skills.
3 To evaluate lecturers' suggestions about applying critical thinking skills in tourism and hospitality subjects.
4 To develop a strategy to enhance the students' experience.

Rationale

The provision of education and training services for people from overseas has become an increasingly important source of income for certain countries, including the UK (Mazzarol and Soutar, 2002). There is a trend towards the universalisation of the education practices of Western countries, since it is mainly the United States, the United Kingdom, Canada and Australia who are instrumental in the internationalisation of education.

The majority of international students who study for a UK qualification come from Asia and especially from China. The UK's popularity amongst Chinese students has grown since America tightened visa regulations after the terrorist attacks in 2001. The UK has become the most popular destination for Chinese students, ahead of America the previous favourite and Germany, where higher education is virtually free (Bird and Owen, 2004). International, and especially non-EU, students inevitably attract large amounts of attention from educational administrators and academics in such subjects as education, economics, and business.

Chinese students come to the UK with expectations that come from their past experiences in China and – whether they realise it or not – they must learn to adapt to new circumstances in order to succeed academically (Turner, 2006). This includes incorporating priorities formulated by the UK education system and often adapting to new ways of studying and preparing assignments (Lowes, Peters and Turner, 2004). Problems arise when UK academics are confronted with what appear to be differences between the standards and expectations of academic staff and those of the Chinese student (Huang, 2004).

The Chinese style of learning has long been influenced by Confucianism. Confucius's approach to education promotes a number of significant concepts that are still evident in Chinese culture (Redding, 1990). The chief among these is the possibility of perfecting the person through self-cultivation, where it is felt that fundamentally all persons can be educated. In addition, the universality of education, where education is seen as a right for all, regardless of status or class, is an underpinning philosophy. Equally the significance of the role of the teacher is important. In Confucian cultures, the teacher's role is not only to impart wisdom to students but also to act as a moral role model.

Typical Chinese classroom activities are dominated by lectures with limited questioning or discussion, because students prefer not to express their opinions in public (Chan, 1999). Problem-solving ability is also largely neglected with student achievement assessed mainly through written examinations, which are not designed to test ability to work with others and solve practical problems (Huang, 2006). In addition, Chinese students may be more concrete and pragmatic in evaluating ideas than their western counterparts, but they may also suffer from a lack of creativity, as well as being less likely to explore new, unaccustomed directions (Harding, 1997).

The problems are more pronounced when Chinese students arrive at western universities for the first time, where they are faced with learning styles and approaches that are alien to them (Vandermensbrugghe, 2004; Egege and Kutieleh, 2004). However, it should be stated that the underlying educational philosophy does include critical enquiry as part of its core value system (Kim, 2003). Exacerbated by often authoritative political systems, the contemporary result has tended to be that students in some Asian countries including China are in practice discouraged from critical engagement (Turner and Acker, 2002).

Literature shows that in spite of the unitarist knowledge traditions of their home societies, students from China who draw heavily on Chinese educational traditions can compete well with their Anglo-European counterparts, especially in numerate and scientific subjects: the so-called Chinese Learner Paradox (Biggs and Watkins, 2001). Equally difficulties emerge when attempting to evaluate deep- and surface-learning approaches and performance among groups such as Chinese students. Within much of UK higher education, stereotypes about Chinese students persist; especially in the social science subjects where stylistic conventions are intimately integrated into forms of intellectual thought (Brown, 1998). The perceived lack of the capability for critical thinking is frequently indicated as a key factor undermining students' ability to perform successfully, particularly in the context of short, intensive postgraduate programmes. Samuelowicz and Bain (2001) argue that although lecturers acknowledge that the difficulties Chinese students have with critical thinking may stem from cultural differences about styles of education, they continue to ascribe any failures in learning capacity to stylistic and language issues.

The idea that the ability to think critically is required to do well at a university in the UK is widespread, but the concept is vague and does not seem to have the same meaning to all people in every circumstance (Vandermensbrugghe, 2004). There are many strands of thought in both the social and philosophical literature that can be labelled 'critical'. Vandermensbrugghe (2004) divides existing definitions of critical thinking into two categories:

1 The ability to develop a capacity to reason logically and cohesively.
2 The ability to question and challenge existing knowledge and social order.

According to Wacquant (2001 cited in Vandermensbrugghe, 2004) it is necessary to bring these two categories of definition together, so that the capacity to reason logically can be used to broaden critical thinking and allow the freedom to think about the world beyond the restrictions imposed by dominant interpretations of it.

It can be seen that the theory of 'critical thinking' is not clearly defined. Because the concept of critical thinking is very broad and non-specific, it gives no clear indication of what needs to be taught. Egege and Kutieleh (2004) argue that there is an assumption that academics, from whatever background, can reliably ascertain the presence of or lack of critical thinking skills in a piece of work. The lack of clear guidelines makes the general teaching of critical thinking problematic and also makes it difficult for students to know what requirements are entailed in practice.

In the face of the difficulties surrounding critical thinking as a concept, criticising international students for not intuitively being capable of thinking critically is not acceptable practice. It should be noted that critical thinking is also often problematic for Anglo-Saxon students (i.e. Pascarella, 1999; Daley et al, 1999), despite their having the advantage of a better understanding of the language and context (Egege and Kutieleh, 2004; Turner, 2006).

Study

To investigate this further, a combination of data collection methods was chosen. In-depth interviews were used as they combine the flexibility of the unstructured interview with the comparability of key questions. The following two questions were asked of students:

1 What is your perception of critical thinking?

2 What kind of difficulties do you have when you apply critical thinking in your study?

Eight students were interviewed between February and April 2006.

Focus group discussion allows a number of respondents to be gathered in one place and time, to discuss a specific topic, under the guidance of the researcher. As the lecturers are all in the author's group and this group tends to have lunch together, it was very convenient for questions to be asked at that time. Each individual was free to agree, disagree, question, and discuss the issues with others in the room. As such it was clear that it was likely that focus group discussions could be used to meet most of the data requirements of the research. In May 2006, two focus group discussions involving eight lecturers were organised at which two questions were put forward:

1 In your mind, what does critical thinking mean?
2 How do you apply critical thinking in your work?

A few observation sessions were also conducted in order to get an insight into the experience of some Chinese students when they are applying critical thinking skills. This also allowed information on the subjects' real problems and issues to be collected, unlike non-participant observation. When the students were observed, the researcher always bore in mind the question, 'What kind of difficulties do the students have when they are doing their assignments with requirement of critical thinking?'

Data analysis overlapped with data collection to build a coherent interpretation. Using a manual process, the researcher made an interview transcription immediately after each interview and carried out the analysis simultaneously. Strauss and Corbin's microanalysis (1998), a line-by-line analysis to generate initial categories and to discover the relationships among concepts was used.

Findings

The researcher interviewed 10 Chinese students and all eight of their lecturers. The interviews conducted during the study are numbered CIS1–10 and also L1–8. Throughout the discussion of the results, these numbers are given in brackets following each excerpt. The profile of interviewed Chinese students and also their lecturers is shown Table 1 and 2.

Table 1   Profile of Chinese students interviewed

Code (CIS)	1	2	3	4	5	6	7	8	9	10
Gender	F	F	F	F	F	F	F	M	M	M
First degree in English (y/n)	Y	Y	Y	Y	Y	N	N	N	N	N

Table 2   Profile of lecturers interviewed

Code (L)	Gender	Years in teaching	Subject groups
1	M	20	Tourism
2	M	17	Tourism
3	M	14	Tourism
4	M	10	Tourism
5	M	10	Hospitality
6	M	12	Hospitality
7	F	8	Tourism
8	F	5	Hospitality

The students' perceptions of critical thinking

As far as the students' perceptions of critical thinking are concerned, different views were identified. Their views fall into the following three categories:

1 Critical thinking means thinking about the advantages and disadvantages of every theory used

Based on their experiences of their undergraduate studies in the UK, four interviewees summarised that critical thinking means thinking about the pros and cons of theories or findings that they have used. The following quotations from the transcripts reflect their understanding:

> 'After finishing my degree in business management here, critical thinking in my mind means advantages and disadvantages of theories you used'. (CIS 4)

> 'I clearly remember that my lecturer told me that critical thinking means thinking critically, that is positive and negative side of every story you heard'. (CIS 5)

2 Critical thinking means being critical of the research process

Two interviewees discussed their understanding of critical thinking based on their experiences of writing their independent projects during the final year of their study for a degree. They recalled that their lecturers told them that critical thinking means doing things logically, and placing emphasis on the research process. They stated the following:

> 'Originally I was not sure of the meaning of 'critical thinking'. But after discussing the matter with my supervisor, I got an idea that to be critical meant thinking and writing in a logical manner, and also reasoning every action I take'. (CIS 3)

> 'At the beginning I thought that critical thinking meant to criticise the theories you used or findings you got. But my supervisor told me that the emphasis is on the research process.' (CIS 6)

3 I don't understand what critical thinking means

Because of a lack of knowledge or practice in the skill of critical analysis, two post-graduate interviewees who were 'direct entry' students from China, felt confused and depressed. For example:

'I have been told by my supervisor that my work lacks critical analysis. I really don't know what critical analysis means.' (CIS 1)

'When I began writing my dissertation I did not have a clear understanding of the skills required to write from a critical approach, I really suffered when I read my supervisor's feedback about my literature review. I thought I did a good job, but my supervisor asked me where my opinion was.' (CIS 2)

The students' difficulties on applying critical thinking in their studies

When the students were asked what kind of difficulties they had when applying critical thinking in their studies, their concerns and anxieties can be summarised as follows:

1 Language barriers

A majority of students reported that they understand what critical thinking means but their English language skills are insufficient for them to apply critical thinking in their coursework or exams. As two interviewees frankly admitted:

'I don't think my English is good enough for postgraduate studies. I am struggling to read books and journal articles that lecturers recommended… being critical, I need to read a lot of materials but my English really stops me being critical' (CIS 8)

'Being critical means I can construct my arguments logically. But I can't as my vocabulary and grammar skills are not good enough to form clear sentences. Most of time I know how to argue in Chinese but not in English' (CIS 6)

2 Lack of clear understanding of critical thinking

Several students also complained that because of their unclear understanding of critical thinking, they find it very difficult to apply it in their coursework.

'Different lecturers tell me different things when I ask them what critical thinking really means. These really confuse me when I write my assignments.' (CIS 9)

'As I have never been told by any lecturer how to apply critical thinking to my study, I am not sure whether I used it when I wrote my assignments. Low marks for my coursework possibly mean I did not use it.' (CIS 1)

As the author is the international student tutor for the Business School and also a lecturer on the Tourism and Hospitality Management programme, she was always consulted when the Chinese students were preparing their assignments for different modules. The findings from the authors' participant observations of four Chinese students when they were preparing their assignments for two different modules (*Tourism – Modern Synthesis* and *Research Methods*) are very similar to the results from the semi-structured interviews.

Although the four students obtained their undergraduate degrees from the UK, they were still unfamiliar with the concept and application of critical thinking in their work. This can be supported by the students' observation on their marks for their assignments. The four students said that though they prepared their assignments in a similar fashion to those in their undergraduate studies, they got a much lower mark for their masters' assignments. The students complained that their lecturers took it for granted that students knew what critical thinking means. As they have never been taught how to apply critical thinking in their studies, they were very unsure what was required. They reported that they had applied critical thinking according to their own understanding.

The lecturers' perceptions of critical thinking

The research findings issuing from discussions with the eight lecturers involved in teaching the postgraduate degree in Tourism and Hospitality management are interesting, as the lecturers hold different views on critical thinking.

As Lecturers 1 and 2 are responsible for the *Research Methods* module, their emphasis on the students' logical research process is obvious, shown by their statements below:

'For me, critical thinking means you can develop your argument logically and cohesively.' (L 2)

'You can easily find definitions from textbooks about critical thinking. Critical thinking means thinking critically on the research content and also the research process to produce the content you read.' (L 1)

Lecturer 3 is the module leader for *Tourism – Modern Synthesis*. This module is an introductory module to this subject area for masters students, which emphasises different theories used in different sub-sectors of the tourism industry. Lecturer 3's statement below reflects the aim of the module clearly:

'When I assess students' assignments, critical thinking means broad reading and critical discussion on different theories and findings.' (L 3)

Lecturers 5, 6 and 8 are all involved in the *Strategic Hospitality Management* module. For them, although there are some differences in terms of wording, their understanding of critical thinking is similar to that of Lecturer 5:

'When I ask students to be critical, it means you should not just copy what others say but also make some comments. Yet your comments need some evidence to support them.' (L 5)

The lecturers' solutions for the students

The researcher asked whether the lecturers outline the procedures for the students to follow when applying the process of critical thinking in their studies. The lecturers agreed that critical thinking is a cultural practice instead of a universal practice so, because the Chinese students have a different cultural background to their lecturers, they should be encouraged to learn a different way of thinking. In terms of procedures for the students to follow, the lecturers are very careful to add to each other's lists.

'I think that when students apply critical thinking to their studies, they should read a broad range of research materials about the topic that they are studying, then they should identify the opinions offered by different authors. Finally, the students should develop their own opinions together with the students' reasons for that opinion.' (L 3)

'This requires a self-conscious reflection on the process of critique and the subsequent construction of knowledge claims, using a specific kind of argumentation.' (L 2)

'Including critical thinking in their work requires the students to show a broad and in-depth understanding of the topic, and then clearly argue their own opinion on the topic researched'. (L 4)

Overall, both the students and the lecturers have different views on critical thinking. The students' problems with the application of critical thinking are due to their language barriers and also their unclear understanding of the skill of critical thinking. The lecturers tend to have different emphases on research content or research process. In terms of solutions provided by the lecturers, common threads can be drawn.

Discussion

The research findings suggest that the Chinese students have different views on critical thinking. These findings are consistent with the observation of Lowes et al (2004) on the academic experiences of international students in the UK. The finding that language barriers cause problems for students in applying critical analysis follows the findings of Huang (2006) that Chinese tourism and hospitality postgraduates have difficulties in being critical due to insufficient language skills. The students' lack of a clear understanding of critical thinking causes difficulties in application: this is similar to Vandermensbrugghe's (2004) argument that Chinese students experience difficulties when they are faced with approaches that are alien to them. Wong (2004) also supports this argument.

The research findings also reveal that different lecturers have different understandings of critical thinking. These findings reflect Mingers' (2000) conclusion that the concept of critical thinking is vague, and different educators have different views on this matter. The lecturers' consensus that critical thinking is a cultural practice, is broadly supported by researchers in this area (Egege and Kutieleh, 2004; Turner, 2006).

Development

Although the lecturers have different definitions of critical thinking, the solutions provided by them on the application of critical thinking in the students' studies can be summarised in the following steps.

Students coming to study in the UK should:

1 Acknowledge that different cultures have different learning approaches. Critical thinking is an approach used in western societies like the UK to aid knowledge acquisition.
2 Read broadly and in depth on the topic to be researched.
3 Identify different opinions from the reading and construct their own arguments

with self-conscious reflection on the process of critique.

These steps are likely to be beneficial to international students who have difficulties over the use of critical thinking in their studies.

Conclusion

Critical thinking is a vital part of teaching students how to think and write while they are studying at UK universities. Although this is a small-scale project, it offers a Chinese student perspective on critical thinking as a counterbalance to the dominance of the academic perspective and a focus on indigenous students. The research findings suggest that students have different understandings of critical thinking. Due to this lack of clarity and also to language barriers, Chinese students have difficulties in applying critical thinking during their studies. Although the lecturers interviewed have different definitions of critical thinking, what they say could be beneficial to the students and offer some solutions to the problem.

There is significant scope for further research in this area, particularly related to perceptions of critical thinking in Chinese students who are studying other subjects in the UK. In addition, a comparison of Chinese students studying in different countries would be valuable to assess how the perception of critical thinking varies according to location and culture. Equally important, further research into the understanding and application of critical thinking among UK lecturers is needed (or over an even wider geographic area, for example in English-speaking countries). Such research would provide a much needed fuller understanding of critical thinking in general and possibly assist in the provision of better support and advice for all students.

Study limitation

Care must be taken in considering the results of this study as it only included Chinese students on one postgraduate degree in tourism and hospitality management from one university. Therefore the results may not be representative of Chinese students in the UK *per se*, so limiting the general applicability of the study findings.

References

Biggs, J. and Watkins, D. (eds) (2001) *Teaching the Chinese learner: psychological and pedagogical perspectives.* Hong Kong: Comparative Education Research Centre, The University of Hong Kong

Bird, S and Owen, G. (2004) Class divides Chinese who profit in Britain. *The Times*, Friday, 13 February p 12

Brown, K. (1998) *Education, culture and critical thinking.* Aldershot: Ashgate

Chan, S. (1999) The Chinese learner – a question of style. *Education and Training* 41 (6/7) pp 294–304

Daley, B. J., Shaw, C. R., Balistrieri, T., Glasenapp, K. and Piacentine, L. (1999) Concept maps: a strategy to teach and evaluate critical thinking. *Journal of Nursing Education* 38 (1) pp 42–7

Egege, S. & Kutieleh, S. (2004) Critical thinking: teaching foreign notions to foreign students.

International Education Journal 4 (4) pp 75–85

Harding, J. (1997) Business education. *Financial Times* 27 January

Huang, R. (2004) The experience of mainland Chinese international students in the UK: a tourism perspective. Unpublished PhD thesis Derby: University of Derby

Huang, R. (2006) Chinese international students' perceptions on Problem-based learning. *Journal of Hospitality, Leisure, Sport and Tourism Education* 4 (2) pp 36–43

Lowes, R., Peters, H. and Turner, M. (2004) *The international student's guide studying in English at University.* London: Sage

Mazzarol, T. and Soutar, G. N. (2002) 'Push-pull' factors influencing international student destination choice. *The International Journal of Educational Management* 16 (2) pp 82–90

Mingers, J. (2000) What is it to be critical? Teaching a critical approach to management undergraduates. *Management Learning* 31 (2) pp 219–37

Pascarella, E. T. (1999) The development of critical thinking: does college make a difference? *Journal of College Student Development* 40 (5) pp 562–69

Redding, G. (1990) *The Chinese Capitalism.* New York: Walter de Guyter

Samuelowicz, K. and Bain, J. (2001) Revisiting academics' beliefs about teaching and learning. *Higher Education* 41 pp 299–325

Strauss A. L. and Corbin, J. M. (1998) *Basics of Qualitative Research: Techniques and Procedures for Developing Grounded Theory.* Beverly Hills CA: Sage

Turner, Y. (2006) Students from mainland China and critical thinking in postgraduate business and management degrees: teasing out tensions of culture, style and substance. *International Journal of Management Education* 5 (1) pp 3–11

Turner, Y. and Acker, A. (2002) *Education in the New China: shaping ideas at work.* Aldershot: Ashgate

UKCOSA (2005) International student statistics for Higher Education in the UK. www.ukcosa.org.uk/pages/hestats.htm accessed on 25/05/06

Vandermensbrugghe, J. (2004) The unbearable vagueness of critical thinking in the context of the Anglo-Saxonisation of Education. *International Education Journal* 5 (3) pp 417–22

Wong, J. (2004) Are the learning styles of Asian international students culturally or contextually based? *International Education Journal* 4 (4) pp 154–66

RONG HUANG is a lecturer in tourism marketing and an international student tutor at the University of Plymouth (UK). Her teaching interests focus on introduction to tourism, tourism and hospitality marketing, and also heritage tourism. Her research interests include student travel, food tourism and tourism education. Rong has been awarded the Prime Minister's Initiative Pilot Project Award and also Higher Education Academy HLST Network funding for a pedagogical research and development project around facilitating the experience of international students in the UK.

14

More than study
Exploring relationship-building with overseas students

Mike Lowe
Manchester Metropolitan University

Seeing the international-student experience as a customer journey, Mike Lowe uses the ideas of relationship marketing to throw light on group dynamics, cultural expectations and challenges. Like all relationships, it's a two-way process.

This chapter illustrates how relationship marketing can influence programme development and delivery. Relationship marketing is a process that is created by an organisation to develop and maintain enhancement of value over time (Kotler, Armstrong, Saunders & Wong, 1996). We chose to use relationship marketing to illustrate developments in the relationship between academics and cohorts of Hong Kong (HK) students studying on Manchester Metropolitan University's BA (Hons) Leisure Management Extension Degree programme. Changes within this relationship have led the programme team to a greater understanding of the needs of Hong Kong students, both academic and non-academic, which they have sought to address. Relationship marketing is enhanced through trust-based long-term relationships (Trim, 2003) and it in this context that the chapter ends with an illustration of future curriculum developments arising from the maturing relationship.

Objectives

The objectives for this chapter follow a timeline by exploring the relationship between programme tutors and HK students from pre-programme entry, through programme delivery to post-programme and are, more specifically:

○ To provide an insight into relationship development between HK students and programme tutors.

○ To illustrate differences in relationship building between HK students and programme tutors and HK tutors.

○ To analyse the programme tutor–HK student relationship legacy after completion of the programme.

○ To illustrate how post-programme relationships can influence programme delivery mechanisms.

Rationale

Overseas student recruitment has always been a mainstay of Manchester Metropolitan University's (MMU) recruitment strategy. The university's strategic plan alludes to having 'grown its share of international students' (MMU, 2008). Apart from the financial benefits in programme and accommodation fees, overseas students bring a wealth of cultural experiences that can be used by tutors to enrich programme design and delivery. However, failure to draw upon the cultural experiences of overseas students and allowing content and delivery to remain UK-centric may result in disengagement or division.

Competition within the university sector for overseas students is based to a large extent on institution and subject rankings which are important marketing tools for recruiters. While these are pivotal in attracting overseas students, they provide no real indication of the overseas student experience after enrolment. It is suggested that these rankings should be seen as the tip of the relationship-marketing process.

A process to recognise the wealth of experiences that overseas students bring with them, as far as is practical, should be used within programme delivery and then design. Student experience while studying in the UK can and will play an increasingly important part in the marketing of programmes. As part of this experience the relationship with programme peers and programme tutors is pivotal and as Kotler et al suggest 'creating, maintaining and enhancing ... building value laden relationships' (1996: 450) is an essential ingredient of relationship marketing.

Against this backdrop, this chapter undertakes an analysis of relationship building between HK students and programme tutors on one academic undergraduate programme – BA (Hons) Leisure Management Extension Degree at MMU – and illustrates how the importance of such relationships can prove to be more than just a marketing tool.

Context

In May 2001 the BA (Hons) Leisure Management suite of programmes was validated for a September 2001 start. The programmes included the BA (Hons) Leisure Management Extension Degree which is a one-year top-up degree (Figure 1):

Figure 1   Graduate skills for leisure management

Level 3	Leisure and Recreation Management	Contemporary Leisure Issues	Visitor Management Project	Strategic Management	Leisure Marketing
	20 credits	20 credits	20 credits	20 credits	20 credits

BA (Hons) Leisure Management Extension Degree (source: *MMU Leisure Studies* definitive Document 2001 p 10)

A feature of this programme was the unit *Graduate Skills for Leisure Management* which serves as a bridging unit between level 2 and 3 (now level 5 and 6) but is assessed as a level 3 (level 6) final year unit. The delivery of this unit is intensive over a one-week period and is timetabled one week before first-year students start the academic year, during which three assessed activities are undertaken. The remaining assessments are usually completed by the end of the first term.

As part of the validation process and, as a result of a previous visit by representatives from City University (CityU) of Hong Kong, a memorandum of understanding was developed that enabled students graduating from CityU's associate degree in Community Service Management (CSM) to progress onto the BA (Hons) Leisure Management extension degree programme (subject to relevant academic and English language achievement).

The start … critical incidents!

The first cohort of seven HK graduates from the associate degree in CSM arrived in September 2001. They were transported from Manchester Airport in a minibus and dropped at the Crewe Campus of MMU to be met by two programme tutors. It was immediately evident from the start that the team were ill-prepared for the arrival of overseas students. This was due in part to a lack of internal communication and in part to little understanding and experience of the needs of such students within the team. As a result, this first cohort of HK students faced the following obstacles:

- no bedding
- no food
- no catering facilities
- closure of refectory and most student campus facilities
- no knowledge of the locality.

This first point of contact was a disaster. Bitner (1990) suggests that clients often judge the perceived quality of their experience through the interaction and evaluation of the servicescapes [physical environment]. The only saving grace in this instance was that the HK students could be seen as a 'captive audience' (with few alternatives) and so there was time to change the initial overwhelming negative perceptions. This and the fact that relationship marketing is a trust-based long-term development (Baron and Harris, 1995; Trim, 2003) meant that we had an opportunity to change initial perceptions over the academic year.

To overcome most of the initial obstacles, programme tutors accompanied the students to the local shops – as campus facilities were closed. At the time we saw this course of action as necessary to rectify our failings, but the HK students found the fact that programme tutors participated in these non-academic activities extremely surprising, reflecting cultural differences in their perception of academic tutors. It was recognised much later that this activity was instrumental in initial relationship and trust-building with the first HK student cohort.

The following day (Sunday) the UK students arrived at the campus and took up residence in the same halls as the overseas students. On Monday, all students started their studies.

The first cohort of leisure management extension degree students consisted of 21 students: five from Ireland, nine from England and the seven HK students. As with most groups, students are readily identifiable by specific characteristics – loud ones, quiet ones, jokers and rare attendees – and while these do not fall precisely within Belbin's group-dynamic classifications, they are prevalent in group formulation and function. The team expected that UK students could be classified by these roles; it was not expected that HK students would follow the same pattern. With the exception of one (a joker) the remaining roles could be classified as – quiet ones, 'only answer when directly asked' ones and very quiet ones. The joker was the exception as HK academic culture is that education is a serious matter. There is a belief that the tutor is always right, the 'font of all knowledge' and should not be questioned.

This culture came into conflict with the ethos of the leisure management extension degree programme, which has always been to encourage autonomy, independent thought and learning. This is reflected in the programme assessments which give students the opportunity to mould their assessments around a possible career orientation. It was problematic for HK students (but not UK-based students) to become autonomous learners and this showed in the *Visitor Management Project* (dissertation) [see Figure 1]. Tutors ask students to develop a proposal based on their choice of 'leisure-related topic area'. HK students had great difficulty in developing their topic areas and with one exception (the joker), tended to agree with the first suggestion made by their project supervisor.

HK students have a particular cultural view and expectations of their tutors, and this conflicts with the UK cultural view. UK tutors see their role as *supervisors* and *facilitators* of learning and teaching for all units, placing the onus on students to undertake independent study on their topic. HK tutors are *instructors* for all aspects of learning and teaching including projects and dissertations. HK tutors expect HK students to follow their instruction without question. So here we place a demand on HK students studying in the UK to change their learning style.

Cultural differences reflect different learning styles but they are also, in some cases, the motivation for HK students to study in the UK, to learn more about UK culture and to immerse themselves in this culture. In acknowledging and responding to this the programme team developed what can be now termed as an enculturalisation process, refined since the first cohort. With the first cohort, the enculturalisation process was ad hoc and consisted of a variety of activities throughout the academic year – visits and activities relating to 'traditional Englishness' (Bonfire night, Alton Towers, Jodrell Bank, historic buildings, local villages complete with thatched-roof buildings) which, as we learned from student feedback, fell short of their expectations.

Baron and Harris (1995) however, point to the fact that satisfaction is not only transaction-specific but also cumulative over a period of time. So once again, as with the initial arrival, when these activities failed to deliver, the programme team had to improve on the quality of the whole experience over the remaining academic year.

Happily, the traditional Christmas meal complete with paper hats and Christmas crackers proved to be a hit with the first cohort and also for subsequent cohorts.

Building the relationship

HK students also gain UK cultural experience by obtaining part-time employment. Their varied motivations are to improve English-language skills, to earn income, to gain experience of working in another country and to build their CV. The first cohort of HK students possessed good language skills and did not feel the need to earn an income. Although they agreed that obtaining work experience would improve their CV, they balanced this benefit against the academic demands of their one-year programme and subsequently decided against undertaking part-time employment.

The festive season is a time that needed more consideration than we initially gave. Again through a lack of understanding, experience and communication, remedial action had to be taken with the first cohort of HK students at the Christmas break. UK students went home for the Christmas period and four of the HK students embarked on European travel, leaving three students on their own in halls of residence over Christmas. It became evident in the last week of the academic term that these three HK students would have very few facilities available, as the campus would again be closed over the holiday.

The relationship built with the HK students was open and honest, and the students knew that whilst the programme team were novices with respect to meeting the needs of overseas students (confirmed by their friends studying at other UK universities), they were responsive in meeting their needs and requests.

But the three HK students who remained in halls over Christmas were unwilling to inform the programme tutors of their plight, as they did not want to burden the tutors with non-academic problems. It was only by accident that programme tutors became aware of these students. The action taken might seem to be above and beyond the call of duty, but one tutor invited the students for Christmas dinner and to stay overnight. This act had a lasting effect not just on the three, but on all seven of the first cohort of HK students and in terms of relationship building was dramatic. 'Social benefits including emotional satisfaction, spiritual values and the sharing of humanitarian ideals' are key features of the relationship marketing process (Arnett el al, 2003: 91).

In all years, and in contrast to the Christmas break, the Easter period signifies an end to class-contact time and the completion of all assessed work. The reactions of HK students and UK students leading up to the Easter break are quite distinctly different. UK students become stressed, thinking that they will not have all the work in by due deadlines, while HK students appear confident in meeting all deadlines, including their project, which can be attributed to their good time-management and work ethos.

After the Easter holiday and before the graduation ceremony, HK students tend to travel, exploring new cultures around Europe before returning in July for graduation. The first cohort of HK students not only invited their families to attend the graduation ceremony but also arranged accommodation for their guests. Whether this was because they saw it as a personal matter or whether it was as a direct consequence of their experiences on arrival in the UK is uncertain. It is probably the former rather than the latter as subsequent cohorts of overseas students have also arranged accommodation for their families for their graduation.

The first cohort of seven HK students graduated in July 2002. Five achieved an upper second and two a lower second. It was evident that the HK students had outperformed many of their UK counterparts, a remarkable achievement given the short duration of the programme, cultural differences and everything else they experienced!

The here and now … size matters

Since the first arrival, there have been three more cohorts of HK students studying on the BA (Hons) Leisure Management extension degree. Programme tutors have reflected on early experiences with the aim of developing and enhancing relationships (Payne and Ballantyne, 1991) and of improving the experience of subsequent cohorts. To some extent this has been successful. However, new groups have also brought new challenges, exposed further naïveties and tested the early initiatives developed to assist overseas students. Specific issues relate to the dynamics of learning and teaching groups and the enculturalisation process, and are detailed below.

The second cohort of HK students numbered 12 and represented 50% of the total intake. The initial problems encountered by the first cohort were overcome with planning and the appointment of a member of the programme team as international welfare officer. Having a member of the teaching team with an understanding of the needs of HK students and with experience of the previous year's problems enhanced the relationship marketing process.

The international welfare officer visited HK to recruit and prepare students for study in the UK. Using 'the joker' from the previous year's cohort to present programme information provided potential applicants with a HK student's view of what was to come, a 'warts and all' perspective, more than just 'programme promotion'.

The problems associated with the arrival of students at the campus, registering with the relevant authorities (such as police, doctors), details on campus closure times and vacation periods, were addressed at the start of the programme. Integrating the enculturalisation process with the faculty overseas orientation programme helped meet the needs of the second and subsequent cohorts.

In later cohorts group dynamics became an issue in two ways. The second cohort replicated the characteristics of the first one – the joker, quiet ones, those who only answer when directly asked and very quiet ones – with the majority of this cohort falling into the latter categories. Despite the size of the cohort, student interaction was limited, with many students remaining silent and hiding within the HK group. The HK cohort was large enough to hide in. It became increasingly difficult to build relationships with this second cohort, in contrast to the first group where all seven students had become proactive during seminars and tutorials. The second cohort relied on four or five members to talk in seminars and attend small group (three or four) tutorials instead of individual group tutorials. Many chose to be absent from these. This led to two distinct sub-groups within the second cohort; one a proactive, responsive group, resembling the first cohort and the second a reclusive, reluctant group.

Despite the programme team's efforts to improve the experience the 'whole group' experience was not as enjoyable as that of the first cohort. Subsequent groups consisted of two or three HK students – the distinctiveness of a cohort that represented 30% or 50% of the total group is lost when the cohort represents only 8% of the total. However, in smaller seminars and tutorials two or three HK students, who might be lost in a larger group setting, can contribute more. The later groups graduated with similar success to the first cohort with upper and lower class second classifications equally split.

Many authors have reinforced the fact that relationship marketing is enhanced through the development of 'workable, trust-based long-term relationships which meet customer expectations' (Morgan and Hunt, 1994; Palmer, 1995; Gronroos, 1997; Chee and Harris, 1998, in Trim, 2003: 563–4). In following this ethos, the programme team have developed long-term relationships with a number of HK universities but the relationships with student cohorts vary.

The first cohort set the pattern for the relationship during the running of the course, but although subsequent groups generally reflected this pattern, there was one major difference between them and the first course. The good relations with the first group outlived the course and continued, whereas later groups did not maintain the relationship with the course team.

This suggests that most relationships formed for the duration of the programme i.e. 'on-course' relationships serve a specific purpose – they are academic and programme-orientated. While 'on-course' relationships that have continued beyond the programme have developed into more socially orientated relationships, which Gummesson (2002: 147) suggests from a relationship marketing perspective are 'pivotal' and the 'most stable part of business life'.

This is clearly illustrated by the fact that regular if distant, contact has been maintained with five of the seven students from the first cohort. These five students have since continued their studies to masters level and have subsequently secured employment. Four of them are employed by Hong Kong Leisure and Cultural Services Division.

The future ... full circle

The memorandum of understanding with CityU was replaced with an articulation of progression and this was expanded to a number of CityU programmes as well as to other Hong Kong universities.

Yet despite this and a number of recruitment visits over the last four years, there has been decline in numbers of HK students studying on the BA (Hons) Leisure Management Extension Degree programme. The main reasons cited for this decline in numbers are financial – cost of tuition, cost of accommodation, living expenses and strong sterling (the current year excluded). As a result of the declining numbers and to comply with the university's strategic focus on increasing numbers of overseas students, the programme team is re-evaluating the course.

As part of the relationship marketing enhancement process, one of the members of the first group from HK (the joker) has been recruited as a departmental ambassador to promote leisure management related programmes to HK students. This ex-student is chairperson of the CityU alumni and is currently working as a sports development manager for the Hong Kong Leisure and Cultural Services Department

The delivery of leisure-related top-up degree programmes in HK was discussed during recent dialogue with one of the HK partner universities. Traditionally this method of delivery includes mechanisms like distance learning and blocked on-site delivery. However as a direct result of the relationship developed with the first cohort of HK students, and the continued relationship with five of these students, a new method of delivery is being devised, drawing on the experiences of past HK students. As the first cohort of students are qualified at masters level in relevant disciplines and are all currently employed within the leisure industry the proposed on-site delivery will include input by members of this cohort.

The advantages of including members of the first cohort in the delivery of an on-site programme are that they:

○ are MMU leisure management graduates and understand the philosophy of leisure-related programmes
○ have a knowledge of quality assurance procedures within MMU
○ are practising industry-related managers
○ will provide a HK context to programme delivery
○ can and will influence programme development
○ have a knowledge and understanding of higher education in both HK and the UK
○ have a knowledge and understanding of leisure-related employment within HK.

If the proposal comes to fruition then it will be as a direct result of a relationship-marketing approach that was built, developed and enhanced over a seven-year period, covering organisation-focused relationships (student/tutor), social relationships (ex student/tutor) and returning to organisational focused relationships (tutor/colleague).

Evaluation

There are several factors worthy of note drawn from the experiences we have been through:

○ The size of the overseas cohort is important when considering group dynamics and the integration of overseas students with UK based students. The number (seven) of the first cohort of students represented 30% of the total group (21). This first group were large enough to be instrumental in shaping group dynamics yet small enough to prevent fragmentation or the sub-grouping of HK students into those who shied away from integration and those who sought integration. This happened in the second cohort (12) who represented 50% of the total group size.

○ Starting the academic programme one week before any other students arrive without a doubt aids the acclimatisation of overseas students and later their integration with UK students. The intensity of the first week of the programme (the *Graduate Skills for Leisure Management* unit) means all students are together for six hours in class each day.

○ The fact that all students live in the same halls of residence means that bonds are formed from the start of the programme. These bonds are strengthened not only by studying together for long periods of time but by living and socialising together.

○ The introduction of assessed group activities during the first week of the programme has the benefit of encouraging (or enforcing) integration. The common goal of achievement, success and a high mark provides a focus for all students.

○ The initial meeting with programme tutors on arrival at the institution provides overseas students with information about their perceived value. The fact that tutors are seen to be giving up their time to assist with non-academic activities can be a contrast to previous academic experiences in their home country. This perception can be further enhanced by programme tutors becoming involved with orientation and enculturalisation activities.

○ Overseas students should not only take part in the enculturalisation process, they should also inform the process, which should be seen as continuous and include university and faculty orientation activities. Opportunities should be made available for overseas students to immerse themselves in English culture and should include the opportunity to undertake volunteer activities or part-time employment.

Conclusion

Relationship marketing is essential in the development and enhancement of relationships with customers (Baron and Harris, 1995). Trim (2003) suggests that universities should adopt a strategic approach to relationship marketing as a means of positioning themselves in overseas markets. The above illustration does not represent a strategic or coherent approach to relationship marketing but provides an insight into the benefits of developing and enhancing relationships over a period of seven years. A direct result of this relationship is the modification of academic programme delivery to overseas students.

References

Arnett, D.B., German, S.D. and Hunt, S.D. (2003) The "identify salience" model of relationship marketing success: the case of non-profit marketing. *Journal of Marketing* **67** pp 89-105

Baron, S. and Harris, K. (1995) *Services Marketing Texts and Cases.* London: Macmillan Press

Bitner, M. (1990) Evaluating Service Encounters: The effect of Physical Surroundings and Employees Responses. *Journal of Marketing* pp 69-82

Gummeson, E. (2002) *Total Relationship Marketing* 2nd ed. Oxford: Butterworth-Heinemann

Kotler, P., Armstrong, G., Saunders, J. and Wong, V. (1996) *Principles of Marketing.* Hemel Hempstead: Prentice Hall

MMU (2008) *The 2020Vision Institutional Strategic Plan 2007–2020.* http://www.mmu.ac.uk/news/publications/strategic-plan

MMU (2001) *Leisure Studies Definitive Document.* Crewe: Manchester Metropolitan University

Payne, C. and Ballantyne, D. (1991) *Relationship Marketing: Bringing quality, customer service and marketing together.* Oxford: Butterworth-Heinemann

Trim, P. (2003) Strategic Marketing for further and higher educational institutions: Partnership arrangements and Centres of Entrepreneurship. *The International Journal of Educational Management* **17** (2/3) pp 59–7

MIKE LOWE is a Senior Lecturer and Programme Leader (Leisure Management) within the Department of Exercise and Sport Science at Manchester Metropolitan University. With over 20 years teaching experience in FE and HE, he has developed Leisure Management programmes and taught across a wide range of leisure related subjects. His current research and academic focus reflect skill development, PDP/CPD, employability and reflective practice within leisure, which provide 'added value' to programmes for both UK and overseas students and are the basis of this chapter.

15

The Chinese cultural experience
Year 3 British students visit Zhejiang Gongshang University, China

Sandra King
North East Wales Institute of Higher Education[§]

This chapter outlines the lessons and challenges of our visit, the experience of our two main activities on the visit: learning about Chinese business and speaking English to Chinese students, and the implications for other UK universities.

Objectives

During the first two weeks of November 2006, a group of twenty students and two members of staff from the business school at North East Wales Institute of Higher Education (NEWI) in Wrexham embarked on a study visit to China. The delegation was invited to stay at Zhejiang Gongshang University (ZJGSU) near Hangzhou in eastern China to take part in a programme of activities which were designed to benefit both institutions.

The visit included two elements:

○ An educational programme, delivered in English to the NEWI students, on Chinese culture and business.
○ A *Spoken English Promotion Project* (SEPP) which was designed to engage the NEWI students in English conversation with small groups of Chinese students.

The NEWI cohort of students included a number of final-year undergraduate business students as well as students from other disciplines. All the students were expected to take part in the educational programme and undertake the assessment.

Students on the final year of the business degree programme were required to study a core module of international business during semester one. The China visit provided some of these students with the opportunity of studying international business at a Chinese university, as an alternative to the course at NEWI. The series of lectures delivered at ZJGSU were negotiated in advance to ensure that the necessary objectives were achievable. The assessment included group presentations and individual reflective comments.

The objective for ZJGSU was to provide small groups of Chinese students with

§ Now Glyndŵr University

an opportunity to engage in English conversation and enhance their vocabulary and knowledge of the English language and culture. The NEWI students were given the role of teaching assistants and it was a requirement that the delegation included enthusiastic, lively and sociable students, in order to maximise the learning experience for the Chinese students (ZJGSU, 2008)

Rationale

Universities across the UK have experienced a growth in the numbers of international students during the last few years, and the number of undergraduate applicants from China for 2008 has increased by 20.5%, to 3,386 (Attwood, 2008). The development of relationships with Chinese universities is high on the UK agenda for recruitment purposes. Understanding the cultural environment of Chinese students could be a key factor in appreciating the background of educational practice which Chinese students bring with them to the UK.

The rapid increase in the number of international students at NEWI has provided the tutors with additional challenges and the increase in students, mainly from India and China, has prompted an urgent need to provide a suitable learning experience for multicultural cohorts of students.

The growing diversity of the student cohort has accelerated the need to internationalise business programmes. Webb (2005) cites a number of definitions from literature concerning internationalisation of the curriculum, but all agree that it is more than providing modules with 'international' in the title.

This opportunity for the NEWI delegation provided exposure to an educational and cultural engagement within a Chinese context. With the probable increase in international students studying business at NEWI in the near future, it is recognised (Ryan and Carroll, 2005) that gaining experiences abroad will provide tutors with an empathetic understanding of different cultures, and will assist in the enrichment of academic and teaching practices.

International students who study at NEWI are provided with additional support in English and study skills alongside their specialist studies. In common with other universities (Warwick, 2007) the sessions on English for academic purposes have had limited success, with some poor attendance and lack of student motivation. The engagement of the NEWI students in the *Spoken English Promotion Project* at ZJGSU provided an opportunity to investigate an alternative approach to improving the English levels of Chinese students.

Context

NEWI's mission statement is 'to provide high quality higher education and research in a welcoming, friendly and supportive environment to meet individual, local, national and international needs.' In accordance with other UK universities with similar mission statements, universities are increasingly business driven (Ayoubi and

Al-Habaibeh, 2006) and international partnerships and collaboration have become key corporate objectives.

The visit was organised by the business school and the NEWI delegation was arranged to include two members of the academic staff, nine business students and 11 other students from study disciplines including English, humanities, sound technology, engineering and art.

There were no student cost implications for the tuition, accommodation, food and local travel expenses in China. This element was covered financially by the students' participation in the *Spoken English Promotion Project*. In order to promote the relationship and ensure that the opportunity was available to a cross-section of students, a scholarship arrangement was partially funded by NEWI to pay the airfare.

Description
Preparations for the visit
Following an application process to join the visit, the students were interviewed and selected, based on their suitability, the criteria being set by ZJGSU.

The organisation of arrangements for the visit was a time-consuming task: booking flights, arranging visas, insurance, risk assessment, application forms for ZJGSU, providing detailed fact sheets and declaration forms for students on health, safety and conduct. The students each contributed £120 to the cost of the visit, and although the flight was paid for by NEWI, additional money was required to cover the cost of a visa as well as weekend excursions. This non-refundable contribution was considered appropriate to ensure commitment from the students.

Life on campus
On arrival the NEWI students and staff met other delegations from the Philippines and Chile who were also staying at ZJGSU. The Chinese hosts showed great pleasure and pride in providing a tour of the campus, and a number of official photographs were taken to celebrate the occasion.

The teaching and campus facilities were of a relatively high standard, and were located in a geographical area which contained several other universities outside the city of Hangzhou. The expansion of this university area was apparent, with the construction of a substantial number of impressive university buildings. The NEWI delegation was allocated shared accommodation on the university campus. The rooms were situated together and during the two weeks of the visit this group environment created its own tensions and camaraderie, which was challenging for the tutors to manage.

The students and staff were provided with a 'spending card' which was credited with an amount of money, sufficient to provide living expenses on campus for the two weeks of the visit. Although this credit adequately covered the cost of meals in the student canteen and purchases in the campus shops, both staff and many of the students had difficulty finding food they enjoyed eating. A Kentucky Fried Chicken (KFC) was located within a 20-minute taxi ride, and take-away meals were a welcome purchase on more than one occasion.

Since the NEWI delegation was the only British group of students on campus at that time, the attention aroused was somewhat overwhelming. The relatively tall male NEWI students were an attraction for the female students but also welcome team mates for the male basketball players. British football teams were regarded with interest and formed the basis of many informal discussions between the British and Chinese students.

The student accommodation for the Chinese students was contained within single-sex dormitory blocks, where four students shared a room. With a structured learning environment, long days of study started at 7.30 a.m. and continued late into the evening. Although students were allowed some free time during the day, class-contact time was greatly in excess of that experienced by UK students. English, traditional mathematics and sport were a compulsory element of the curriculum for all students, irrespective of the major subject studied for their degree. It was common practice for Chinese students to read aloud outside during the daytime in order to practise the pronunciation of their English.

Study of Chinese culture and international business

The structure of the morning sessions on Chinese culture and international business followed a traditional lecture approach. The lectures were delivered by Chinese lecturers in English to the NEWI students, alongside other students from Chile and the Philippines. Some sessions were devoted to the Chinese language and culture but others were provided in accordance with previous negotiation on various aspects of international business. The assessment on the return to the UK was based on the lecture sessions and additional information gained from students' own observation and research on aspects of business with China.

Spoken English Promotion Project (SEPP)

The main objective of the visit for ZJGSU was engagement in the *Spoken English Promotion Project* (SEPP). English was high on the agenda for this university and each member of the NEWI delegation was provided with a schedule to meet groups of four Chinese students in the dormitories of study rooms for four hours each weekday. The Chinese students were welcoming and exhibited an enthusiastic attitude to the English sessions. They were eager to learn as much as possible about life in Britain. Although the UK students had previously had no experience of teaching English, the elevation to the status of 'English teacher' provided them with a purposeful sense of achievement.

A printed list of conversation topics, photographs and music were used in the sessions and provided the stimulus for an enthusiastic engagement. The success of the sessions was heightened by the curiosity on the part of both sides about everyday activities and the common interests of young people. The Chinese students gained confidence in oral English and progress was made in forging relationships.

Some of the sessions took place in the gardens on campus rather than in the dormitories as the weather in this part of China in November was often sunny in the afternoons. These outside venues often attracted the attention of other Chinese students who wanted to contribute to, or observe the sessions.

Cultural visits and leisure activities

As part of the pre-arranged package of activities, a coach was provided at the weekends to transport the group to local places of interest. During this time the delegation visited cultural sights and tourist attractions in Hangzhou and Shanghai. The visits also included ample opportunity for shopping, which was a very popular activity for the British students. Some students had not previously experienced the art of price negotiation for purchases, and with the rate of exchange so advantageous for prices, a shopping 'frenzy' gripped the group.

Leisure time was limited during the weekdays as English teaching activities continued until 9pm. Small groups of students often spent the latter part of the evening reflecting on the experiences of the day. On some occasions, activities were arranged on the campus: an outdoor concert, a food fair and a multicultural show which included a performance from the NEWI delegation.

The campus was fairly isolated, but inevitably the British students found a karaoke bar nearby. However, their very late return to the university that night prompted heavy criticism from the Chinese professor.

Attitudes

A very structured timetable of activities was organised for the NEWI delegation and each student and tutor was provided with a schedule for the English project. The programme with the Chinese students was scheduled to finish at 10.30pm and persistent negotiations were required to reduce this time to 9pm. The sessions were scheduled in the dormitory blocks which were spread across a very large campus and there were some concerns from students and staff regarding safety at night. Furthermore, there was uncertainty from some of the NEWI students who were housed in single sex dormitories of the opposite sex. However, since the campus was regarded as a safe environment, the Chinese professors found it difficult to understand the safety concerns expressed by the NEWI delegation.

At ZJGSU it was evident that there was a concerted effort to want to understand and accommodate Western approaches for future exchanges. There was a strong desire to learn, and constructive criticism was welcomed to improve communication and co-operation. Invitations to a Chinese banquet were extended to the tutors at lunchtime on more than one occasion and the exchange of presents was customary.

Rewarding achievement was regarded as very important and the NEWI students were presented with certificates to acknowledge their teaching contribution to the *Spoken English Promotion Project*. The visit has since prompted some of the NEWI students to consider teaching as a career.

Problems encountered

The visit presented some initial difficulties with UK students finding it hard to acclimatise themselves to their new surroundings. There were inevitably some tensions associated with living together in such close confinement for two weeks. Unlike the Chinese students, NEWI students were not used to sharing a room. In advance of the visit, care was taken to allocate rooms to students who were friends with each other, but that was not always possible. Hence, there were some conflicts and tears, but also a lot of shared, valuable experiences.

Campus meals often included body parts of animals which students and staff were not prepared to eat, such as chickens' feet, beaks, fish tails and internal organs. Although the Chinese made extensive efforts to provide suitable alternative food, a number of the students lost a lot of weight. Some relief came with the occasional KFC and restaurant meals at weekends, including both Chinese and Western food.

Students were over-eager to shop for bargains and there were difficulties with overweight cases at the airport on the return to Britain. Stressful negotiations reduced the threat of a large overweight baggage bill to a more manageable amount.

Evaluation

The staff and students from NEWI experienced an insight to the study life at a Chinese university. In comparison with British students, they felt that the Chinese students had limited privacy and freedom; four students sharing a room with no computers allowed during the first study year, no visitors of the opposite sex in dormitories, 'lights out' at 11am and permission required to leave the campus at weekends.

The study visit provided an exhausting but rewarding experience for the UK students and lecturers. Engagement with the Chinese students often extended beyond the English sessions, with basketball games, food tasting and socialising. Students from both nationalities were inquisitive about each other's everyday life and the visit developed significant cultural awareness in the NEWI delegation.

Very few of the NEWI students had previous experience of teaching and this challenge offered them a career prospect which they might not have considered before the visit. The students were invited to return to work in China as English teaching assistants, and although no one has yet taken up this opportunity, subsequently a number of them have decided to pursue a career in teaching. On return to the UK, the ensuing presentations and students' reflective comments showed an appreciation of a population whose eagerness to learn was impressive. The assessment was a core study element for the business students, but there was some dissatisfaction with the lack of effort from the non-business students within the groups, who were awarded a certificate for this additional study. Separate groups of business and non-business students might have been a better option for the group work.

All activities were well organised and the success of the visit was attributable to the preparatory work at NEWI and at ZJGSU. Although the visit included some sightseeing activities at weekends, the long working hours during the weekdays provided a very demanding schedule. One of the original intentions was for NEWI tutors to engage in discussion with the Chinese professors with regard to future engagements and progression of relationships. However, this was not possible; partly due to lack of time, but also etiquette, where there was some reticence to engage in discussions with female tutors who did not command the authority of head of school or principal.

Discussion

There were no bars or clubs provided for the students on the ZJGSU campus, although alcohol was not forbidden. Social life was confined to the campus with film shows, concerts, food fairs and sporting activities, so the minimal participation by Chinese students in the UK 'social scene' is understandable. British universities need to be sensitive to the different leisure needs of international students.

A firmly structured timetable of activities was arranged for the NEWI delegation and there was little opportunity for any deviation. The forever friendly and pleasant attitude from the Chinese seemed to be genuine, but there was a reluctance to 'lose face' when changes to their plans were requested. It is not surprising that it is sometimes difficult for UK lecturers to really appreciate the problems encountered by Chinese students when their friendly and pleasant exterior can sometimes hide the anxieties they may be experiencing.

This type of interaction between the UK and Chinese students was very successful and could be a useful vehicle for interaction between multinational groups within the UK. English sessions within UK universities are surely not greeted with so much enthusiasm. Although the development of subject-specialist language is essential for achievement within a UK university course, an extended induction activity could involve similar small group discussions with UK and international students on topics of mutual interest. Providing training and funding for the UK students to act as 'student teachers' would raise the profile of the task and might encourage engagement.

The China visit provided staff and students with an opportunity to gain some insight into some of the learning styles and background experiences of Chinese students. The exposure to the Chinese learning environment provided a rich learning experience and helped to promote intercultural communication skills. As Ryan and Carroll (2005) indicate, immersion in the cultural and social experience provides a deeper understanding to cultural awareness which will assist in promoting an integrated approach to study in a multicultural context.

References and URLs

Attwood, R. (2008) Healthy rise in undergraduate applications. *THES* 14th February 2008

Ayoubi, R.M. and Al-Habaibeh, A. (2006) An investigation into international business collaboration in higher education organisations: A case study of international partnerships in four UK leading universities. *International Journal of Educational Management* 20 (5) 2006 pp 380–96

Ryan, J. and Carroll, J. (2005) Canaries in the Coalmine: International students in Western universities. In Carroll, J. and Ryan, J. (eds) (2005) *Teaching International Students: Improving Learning for All*. Oxon: Routledge

Warwick, P. (2007) Well Meant But Misguided: A Case Study of an English for Academic Purposes Programme Developed to Support International Learners. *International Journal of Management Education* 6 (2) pp 3-17

Webb, G. (2005) Internationalisation of the curriculum: An institutional approach. In Carroll, J. and Ryan, J. (eds) *Teaching International Students: Improving Learning for All*. Oxon: Routledge

ZJGSU *Spoken English Promotion Project* (SEPP) available from http://www.zjgsu.edu.cn/english/appform.php [accessed 2 April 2008]

SANDRA KING is a senior lecturer in the Business School at North East Wales Institute of Higher Education (NEWI) in Wrexham and is currently programme leader for the business degree programme. Her academic interests include statistical analysis, quantitative methods and research methodology, but she is also involved with the pastoral care and support of students. During November 2006 she organised and led this study visit to China. She was awarded a teaching fellowship in 2007-08 to study and develop an understanding of factors which affect the learning and teaching of international students.

Index